JUDAISM AND
PSYCHOLOGY

JUDAISM AND PSYCHOLOGY
meeting points

AARON RABINOWITZ

JASON ARONSON INC.
Northvale, New Jersey
Jerusalem

This book was set in 11 pt. Bookman by Hightech Data Inc., of Bangalore, India, and printed and bound by Book-mart Press, Inc. of North Bergen, NJ.

Library of Congress Cataloging-in-Publication Data

Rabinowitz, Aaron, 1931–
    Judaism and psychology : meeting points / by Aaron Rabinowitz.
      p. cm.
    Includes bibliographical references and index.
    ISBN 0-7657-6060-6
    1. Judaism and psychology. 2. Psychology, Religious. I. Title.
BM538.P68R33 1999
296.3'71—dc21   98-40643

Printed in the United States of America on acid-free paper. For information and catalog write to Jason Aronson Inc., 230 Livingston Street, Northvale, NJ 07647-1726, or visit our website: www.aronson.com

Contents

Acknowledgments

Portions of this book are extended versions of published articles and chapters. The author gratefully acknowledges the permission granted to him by:

The Plenum Publishing Co., Human Sciences Press, for articles published in *The Journal of Psychology and Judaism*:

"Reflections on the Concept of the Unconscious in Judaism," 4(1), Fall 1979.

"The Unconscious: Its Relation to the Judaism-Psychology Dialogue," 13(3), 1989.

"Human Nature: Thanatos Revisited," 18(3), 1994.

"Psychotherapy: Its Relation to Biblical and Rabbinic Judaism," 21(3), Fall 1997.

The Magnes Press for:

"Values, Morality, and Ethics in Psychology and Religion," in *Sense and Nonsense: Philosophical, Clinical, and Ethical Perspectives*, ed. J. Rozenberg, 1996.

Ktav Publishing House for:

"Psychotherapy and Education," in *Porat Yosef*, eds. B. and E. Safran, 1992.

1

Background

RESEARCH: HISTORY AND PROBLEMS

Humans are consumed and driven by curiosity. People want to understand nature, the environment, social structures, but most of all wish to understand themselves—human nature. Most people evince ardent interest in psychology and this has led to immense progress in furthering scientific psychological knowledge. The difficulties faced by scientists in their task are well documented. It is, however, appropriate to enumerate some of the obstacles encountered by the psychologist–scientist in the quest for deeper and better understanding of the human psyche.

There are difficulties which hamper the psychologist in his search which are not commonly faced by scholars and researchers in other fields. The scientist is first and foremost human and can easily be misled, his/her perception and judgment distorted by the emotional closeness to the subject of the inquiry—human behavior. An ambivalent situation is created, a drive to delve into the reasons explaining behavior, the mysteries of one's nature, which, however, can and do cause anxiety. Dark hidden recesses may be uncovered, which are perhaps better left concealed and not brought into the open to be viewed by all. People, one's own self included, may be portrayed as less than angelic, the darker, more sinister faces of personality may come to the fore—an unpleasant situation one may not wish to face.

Religion is like psychology in that it, too, is emotionally charged. Indeed, it seems to be the subject that, more than any other, evokes intense feelings. History attests to fierce and bloody wars stemming from religious conflicts. Religious beliefs and practices seem to be universal phenomena. This shows that the needs addressed by religion are deep and basic human concerns and characteristics, and indicate why religion is not a topic lightly handled. The study of psychology of religion, touching upon both religion and psychology, is open to the range of emotions associated with both disciplines. Research in this area touching upon the relation between them, their similarities and differences, the possible influence that one may exert on the other, constitute a task to be faced with trepidation. Involving as it does topics fraught with emotion, the scholar needs to be aware that, although he/she wishes to study the topic in a rational manner, there is a real possibility that one may consciously or unconsciously be caught up in a web of emotions and prejudices hampering good judgment. Philip Rieff, in his classic study of Freud, is of the opinion that of the topics discussed by Freud it is on the topic of religion that his analytic reasoning faculties failed him. Rieff writes that Freud used his psychoanalytic tools in open hostility to religion. Rieff feels that psychoanalysis, as articulated by Freud, shows itself to be the last remnant of the secular nineteenth century.[1]

---

1. Rieff, Philip (1970). *Freud: The Mind of the Moralist*, 3rd ed., p. 257. Chicago: The University of Chicago Press.

There is another impediment hampering research in the psychology of religion. Bertocci, the Harvard philosopher who was a close friend of the famed psychologist Gordon Allport, analyzed the psychological interpretations put forth to explain the religious experience.[2] At the onset of his analysis, he discusses the dilemma facing the scientist psychologist. The researcher, he writes, takes as a model the empirical research paradigm used successfully by the physical scientist. Bertocci feels that this premise needs to be questioned. Does, for example, psychological research have to be similar to astronomical research? That research is, of course, based upon objective facts and shuns introspection. Should, he asks, that methodology be followed in research on the psychology of religion? Perhaps the unique requirements of researching the interface of religion and psychology necessitate a different approach? His probing questioning bears explaining. Why has the empirical objective approach lost its charm for him when considering the psychology of religion? Perusal of Bertocci's listing of what he considers pertinent important questions serves to clarify his position. He places understanding the religious experience at the top of his list. This, to him, means addressing the following questions. What is the essence of this experience? Is the experience autonomous, sui generis?—meaning that it can be properly understood only on its own terms, it cannot be interpreted or explained by attempting to find deeper layers upon which the experience is based. This is so because the experience, by definition, is a basic, fundamental phenomenon. Does a religious experience provide a "coming to grips" with reality in such a way which cannot be had or duplicated by other means? Stressing a slightly differ-

---

2. Bertocci, Peter A. (1971). Psychological Interpretations of Religious Experience. *Research on Religious Development: A Comprehensive Handbook,* ed. M. P. Strommen, pp. 5–41. New York: Hawthorn Books.

ent aspect means framing the question thusly: Is the religious experience a continuation of known cognitive and emotional states? It is conceivable, he argues, that the answers to such questions require an approach different from the objective empirical method used in the physical sciences. Perhaps researchers should use the uniquely human traits of introspection and attention to consciousness. Bertocci is well aware of the difficulties involved in such research and discusses them. Psychologists, he writes, identifying themselves as modern scientists, are receptive to methodology based upon the humanistic, naturalistic orientation. They have, however, divorced themselves from the attempt to perceive the human experience as a theological or metaphysical phenomenon. It is true that often they pay lip service and proclaim these points of view to be important, but invariably add that metaphysics and theology must not be permitted to impede the development of psychology into a full-fledged science. Psychologists, as were other scientists, became influenced by the prevailing philosophy extant at the close of the previous century leading them to view the aesthetic, moral, and religious aspects of human nature in biological terms.

The discussion bearing upon the direction, scope, and methodology of psychological research is germane to another development of concern to the topic with which we are dealing. In 1950, Gordon Allport noted that intellectuals, particularly academicians, distanced themselves from the study of religion.[3] He points out that, at the close of the Victorian era, William James allotted a mere two pages in his text to discussing sex, but authored a brilliant work on the religious experience. Commenting on the situation in 1950, he emphasizes that the reverse is the

---

3. Allport, Gordon W. (1950). *The Individual and His Religion,* pp. 1–3. New York: Macmillan Publishing Co.

norm. Psychologists write about the influence sex exerts on human behavior, but remain silent on religious issues. Furthermore, historically this was not so. The end of the previous century that saw the development of psychology as an empirical science, also witnessed emerging interest in the psychology of religion. As early as 1881, the famous American psychologist G. Stanley Hall conducted research on the phenomenon of religious conversion by adolescents.

Allport believes that the reluctance of psychologists in the early and middle twentieth century to study the psychology of religion is rooted in their aim to establish psychology as an empirical science, meaning that research is conducted by formulating hypotheses and testing them experimentally. The psychologists wanted to be accepted by the scientific community on equal terms. They knew that this meant that their research methods must comply with the philosophy, standards, and methodology employed in the physical sciences. This accounted for the decline of interest in the study of the psychology of religion which did not, in that era, lend itself to be studied under those conditions. Allport did not completely negate that attitude, but added that the time for change had arrived. Psychology, he wrote, had matured and been accepted as a bona fide science and does not need to fight for recognition already attained. Others, as well, support his analysis.[4]

The present era has witnessed a radical change and a need is both felt and expressed to examine the religious aspects of behavior psychologically. An imposing body of literature has emerged covering the psychology of religion, some devoted to studying psychological aspects of the religious experience or process, others examining the be-

---

4. Clark, Walter H. (1958). *The Psychology of Religion,* p. 5. New York: The Macmillan Co.

havior of religious people contrasted with nonreligious, a topic perhaps more truly belonging to social or personality psychology. Established journals publish research on these topics, the first founded in 1904.[5] A journal focusing on the specifically Jewish perspective has been introduced and serves to focus and stimulate research.[6]

---

5. The *American Journal of Religious Psychology and Education*. Many major contemporary psychological journals publish studies of religion and religious behavior; for example, *The American Psychologist* and The *Journal of Personality and Social Psychology*. In addition, there are journals devoted specifically to the interface between religion and psychology, for example, *The Journal of Psychology and Christianity* and the *Journal of Psychology and Theology*.

6. *Journal of Psychology and Judaism*.

FACTORS INFLUENCING THE RESURGENCE OF INTEREST IN PSYCHOLOGY OF RELIGION

A factor which has contributed to the resurgence of interest in the topic is the discovery of new and powerful statistical tools that, coupled with computer technology, have greatly expanded the power of research into the psychology of personality. The multiplicity of factors and their complex interrelationships had, in the past, hindered research. This was true for research on the religious behavior of people as well, which, as a result of the new statistical tools and technology, has greatly expanded also.

The emergence of pastoral psychology must be recognized as a major catalyst of renewed interest in the study of religion and psychology. In 1920, Antoin Boisen was admitted to a mental hospital. He recovered, returned to his theological interests, and functioned as a Protestant minister. He published a book in 1936 in which he detailed and described his experiences.[7] He was also one of the founding fathers of pastoral psychology, a movement dedicated to training clergymen to recognize emotional problems, enabling them to cope with the less acute ones and to refer the more difficult cases to professionals. In effect, the functions of the minister are linked to those of the psychiatrist and clinical psychologist, advancing the development of preventive mental health principles. This fruitful relationship has broadened and deepened the dialogue between psychology and religion.

Academic scientific research in religion, a nineteenth century development, has also contributed to renewed interest in the psychology of religion. Psychologists probing the relation between religion and psychology were influenced by the nature, scope, and range of the prob-

---

7. Boisen, Antoin T. (1936). *Exploration of the Inner World,* New York: Harper & Brothers.

lems of interest to scholars studying religion. These developed in two major directions: (a) research into the universal origins of western religions, which included critical analysis of the Bible; (b) an attempt to lay a scientific foundation for a comparative analysis of all religions. Some scholars predicated that there exists a given, a priori base for religion to take root in, which is an integral part of humans, and studied the nature of this given. Others directed their efforts at isolating and defining a common denominator for all religions. There were and are scholars who study the sociological aspects of the changes wrought by the modern world and their effects on the role and perception of religion. For example, the transformation of society from an agricultural community to an industrial one and its effect on religion have been documented.[8]

The noted philosophers of the eighteenth century, Hume, Kant, Lessing, and Schliermacher began to perceive religion as a phenomenon worthy of being studied. This led to the resumption of interest in understanding religion and only then did it become a legitimate branch of philosophy on a par, for example, with the study of ethics.[9] All of the abovementioned new directions and emphases converged to engender renewed interest in the psychological study of religion.

---

8. Marty, Martin E. (1971). Religious Development in Historical, Social and Cultural Context. *Research on Religious Development: A Comprehensive Handbook,* ed. M. P. Strommen, pp. 42–77. New York: Hawthorn Books.

9. Charlesworth, M. J. (1972). *Philosophy of Religion,* Introduction, p. viii. London: Macmillan.

COMMON PREJUDICES OF
THE PSYCHOLOGIST OF RELIGION

Bertocci's comments on the dilemma of the psychologist were noted above. He further analyzes and dissects the influence of what he terms "overbeliefs" of the researcher, by which he means the prejudicial attitudes of psychologists. He is referring to their perception of human nature and the influence this perception may have on their interpretations of the religious aspects of behavior. He reviews and critically analyzes 10 prominent scholars, mostly psychologists, who addressed themselves to the psychology of religion. His conclusion is that their prejudices exerted a powerful influence on their understanding of the religious experience.[10] Another scholar feels that differing evaluations by those studying the psychological implications of religious issues stem from their degree of identification with the particular religion studied or with religion in general. He maintains that religious psychologists favor religious institutions, customs, and experiences, a practice he views with disfavor.[11] He does not, however, discuss the influence of nonreligious or antireligious psychologists on their judgments. In sum, there are two schools of thought. One deems it necessary to warn psychologists of the pitfalls which may befall them if they overidentify with the humanistic-naturalistic train of thought paramount in intellectual circles. This may steer them away from appropriate and legitimate methods of studying religion. The other school of thought feels that the humanistic approach is proper. The possible dan-

---

10. Bertocci, Peter A., ibid.
11. Beit-Hallahmi, Benjamin (1985). Religiously Based Differences in Approach to the Psychology of Religion: Freud, Fromm, Allport and Zillborg. *International Series in Experimental Social Psychology* vol. II, ed. L. B. Brown, pp. 18–33. Oxford: Pergamon Press.

ger to scientific psychological research, according to this line of reasoning, lies in the positive overidentification of psychologists with their subject matter, creating the conditions accounting for what they consider to be the fact that most psychologists who study religion are motivated to do so to defend it from its detractors.

Pruyser[12] and others[13] discuss other aspects of the psychology and religion issue. Pruyser prefers the plural term "psychologies." According to him, psychology of religion has many facets: there isn't one psychology of religion; there are many. The plural usage is meant to focus on diverse issues and theories about this many-faceted subject. He cites socioeconomic, cognitive, behavioral, psychoanlytic, and ego psychology theories as proof of his thesis. He enumerates approximately fifteen major issues researched by psychologists. He sees this complexity as a major determiner of the diverse, and often opposing, theories of the psychology of religion. Furthermore, he argues, the definition of religion, insofar as the interface of psychology and religion is concerned, should not be confined to the classical definition of religion. It should include groups who share identical beliefs, and even individuals who strongly believe in a set of principles should be studied as part of research in the psychology of religion. The complexity of the subject is such that it is not surprising that there are fundamental differences between explanations of the religious experience. This situation calls for not one, but many psychological explanations leading to a pluralistic approach to the psychology of religion.

---

12. Pruyser, Paul W. (1987). Where Do We Go From Here? Scenario for the Psychology of Religion. *Journal for the Scientific Study of Religion* 26:28–34.

13. Vergote, A. (1985). Psychology of Religion as the Study of the Conflict between Belief and Unbelief. *International Series in Experimental Social Psychology,* vol. II, ed. L. B. Brown, pp. 52–61. Oxford: Pergamon Press.

THE AUTHOR'S POSITION AND AIM

Pruyser's perception of what constitutes the issues to be studied by psychologists of religion provides an additional dimension to the previous discussion of the difficulties faced when doing research in this field. He lists seven different motivations for conducting research in psychology of religion. For example, some workers are moved to strengthen religion by pointing to the psychological needs supplied by religion, and some wish to denigrate religion by proving it needless and primitive. He also describes researchers who respect religion, its impact on history, its influence on groups and individuals, its textural richness and many faceted modes of expression. The author basically agrees with this position and this book is an attempt to deal with some issues following this guideline. Although the focus of this work is on Judaism and psychology, the interaction between all religions and psychology will at times be addressed. This is informative in its own right and broadens and deepens the understanding of the threads connecting aspects of Jewish thought, Jewish behavior, and psychological principles. Topics relating to and relevant to both religion and psychology will be analyzed, pointing out common factors and areas of agreement as well as those principles on which their paths diverge.

The language employed in the literature on psychology of religion is divided between terms culled from psychology and those used in theological literature. The topics discussed in this volume are rooted in both disciplines, resulting in language usage that at times is psychologically oriented and at other times bears the mark of expressions and concepts borrowed from Jewish theological literature. Focusing psychological principles on religious issues and applying categories formulated by psychological research and methodology will hopefully lead to new insights in Jewish thought. This is acceptable procedure from the

Jewish point of view. Throughout history talmudists and scholars have uncovered new meanings and fresh nuances in biblical and rabbinical writings. They were aware that the sages declared that new interpretations expounded by gifted students were known to Moses on Mt. Sinai (Babylonian Talmud, Megillah 19B).[14] This dictum justifies new and novel interpretations by teaching that the supposedly new was also given and known to Moses at Sinai. The only rule to be followed is that they be in accordance with the general structure of Torah and Halakha. This allows for creativity in thinking while safeguarding the framework and sanctity of Torah, and exemplifies the unique genius of the sages. In another of their sayings, they likened the discovery of hitherto unknown interpretations of scripture to that of an infant's suckling at its mother's breast in that the infant finds sustenance and pleasure each time (Talmud, Eruvin 54B).

Barbour argues that theology must contend and come to grips with scientific findings on two major issues, creation and the nature of man.[15] The major portion of this work deals with important facets of human nature discussed by both Judaism and psychology. Psychological principles and findings will not be used to seek or discover the theological roots of Judaism. This is not a discourse on theology; consequently, it is not within the scope of this volume to explain the whys of religion. Its aim is to shed light on complex and thorny issues by il-

---

14. There are two sets of Talmud. The first, Talmud Yerushalmi, was compiled in Tiberias. The second, the Babylonian Talmud, is called Talmud Bavli and was compiled at a later date. Its discussions are more extensive and records the opinions of many more scholars and is therefore accepted as authoritative. Henceforth, unless noted otherwise, 'Talmud' will refer to the Babylonian edition.

15. Barbour, Ian G. (1990). *Religion in an Age of Science*, p. xiv. San Francisco: Harper & Row.

luminating religious concepts or behavior from a psychological viewpoint, adding another perspective to Judaic thought.

The issue of reductionism, the tendency to explain religion in terms of concepts not indigenous to religion, is crucial for our discussion. Theories explaining religion and its practice as being rooted in bodily, spiritual, or social human needs—as being a purely human phenomenon formulated by people to address those needs and eliminate a divine factor—are examples of reductionist thinking. Such theories look to psychology, sociology, and allied disciplines to provide an aura of scientific respectability to bolster their claims. Religion, in this view, is not perceived on its own terms, but as an expression of other needs. Classical psychoanalysis is an example of such thinking. Those who oppose reductionism are of the opinion that religion is sui generis, it exists in its own right as an autonomous expression of people's belief that they have a relationship with a transcendent entity. This school insists that religion must be understood on its own terms, its own principles and concepts.[16] In this view it isn't correct to study religion other than the way it presents itself and it is not fruitful to search for other supposedly deeper levels from which it ostensibly flows. It will be recalled that Bertocci argued that religion is sui generis. Eliade, recognized as one of the foremost researchers of the century in the area of comparative religion, accepts as a premise that religion is sui generis,[17] a position held by Hick as

16. Pals, Daniel L. (1987). Is Religion a Sui Generis Phenomenon? *Journal of the American Academy of Religion,* lv: 259–282. See also,

———— (1986). Reductionism and Belief: An Appraisal of Recent Attacks on the Doctrine of Irreducible Religion. *Journal of Religion* 66:18–36.

17. Eliade, Micrea (1958). *Patterns of Comparative Religion,* trans. Rosemary Sheed, p. xi. New York: American Library.

well.[18] The issue of reductionism, touching upon the role of psychology serving as the bedrock upon which all other explanations and interpretations are based, is not unique to the relationship between religion and psychology. Other disciplines as well are subject to the same heated controversy as to the legitimacy and efficacy of viewing their subject matter as manifestations of psychological needs. Anthropologists, for example,[19] are sharply divided whether to apply psychological expertise and knowledge to explain their findings, or to develop a set of concepts and tools intrinsic to their subject matter with which to explain the issues they deal with.[20]

The author has already emphasized that the nature of the confluence of religion and psychology to be explored in this volume is confined to providing fresh insights to religious thought and practice. This means that the issue of religious roots is not the subject matter analyzed. This is congruent with the sui generis perception of religion. However, whatever one's position on the issue of reductionism is, exploring religious thought and behavior by bringing psychological knowledge to bear upon them is, hopefully, a fruitful endeavor.

---

18. Hick, John (1989). *An Interpretation of Religion,* p. 1. New Haven & London: Yale University Press.

19. Bock, Philip K. (1980). *Continuities in Psychological Anthropology,* pp. 131–138. San Francisco: W. H. Freeman & Co.

Heelas Paul (1985). Social Anthropology and the Psychology of Religion. *International Series in Experimental Social Psychology* vol. II, ed. L. B. Brown, pp. 34–51. Oxford: Pergamon Press.

20. Mathematics is generally acknowledged to be the basis of science. It is interesting to note that a physicist (Nick Herbert, *Quantum Reality,* N.Y.: Anchor Press, 1985, p. 2) believes that "although mathematics originates in the human mind, its remarkable effectiveness in explaining the world does not extend to the mind itself. Psychology has proved unusually resistant to the mathematization that works so well in physics." Perhaps this explains why some psychologists feel that their own science is the bedrock on which other disciplines rest.

One final point needs to be made clear. The topics and issues dealt with in this volume do not exhaust the subject matter. They are only some of the issues comprising the interface between religion and psychology. They are major and critical issues, but that does not mean that other topics are less important. The choosing and inclusion of these specific topics reflect the author's interests. It is hoped that they strike a responsive chord in others as well.

Another point to avert misunderstanding. There are two ways of pronouncing Hebrew, Ashkenazic and Sephardic, reflecting the geographical origins of the speaker. Israelis have adopted the Sephardic pronunciation, although many continue to use Ashkenazic pronunciation in prayer. The difference doesn't affect the meaning. It doesn't hinder understanding another's speech. This division has implications when transposing Hebrew into English. For example, "Sayings of the Fathers" can be written "Pirkai Avos" (Ashkenazic) or "Pirkai Avot" (Sephardic). At times, the spelling will follow Ashkenazic custom, at other times Sephardic. The literature contains diverse spellings for certain words, for example: hasidic–hassidic; Kabbalah–Kabalah. Here, as well, at times one spelling will be used and at other times a different custom will be followed.

2

Human Nature

There is no better way to grasp and comprehend Judaism's perception of the psychological forces directing human behavior than to study its conception of human nature. It is a truism that the theories of personality advanced by various schools of psychology reflect the attitudes and prejudices of its proponents and in this respect Judaism is no exception. This chapter deals with a question personality theories and therapeutic systems deal with knowingly or unknowingly: Are people basically good, evil, or neutral? It is not a simple matter to define those terms; however, there seems to be a general consensus as to what they imply, and it is to this general sense that the following arguments and theses are presented.

PSYCHOLOGICAL VIEWS OF HUMAN NATURE; PERSONALITY THEORIES

Psychological theories of human nature are related to and owe their origins to thinkers who through the ages have grappled with this question. People and perhaps entire cultures can be divided into those who believe that man–woman is basically good and those who strongly refute this belief and stress the evil and aggressive facets of human behavior. This polarity is mirrored in psychological theories as well.

Staub[1] sees Rogers and Maslow as believing that man is basically good. He writes:

> Maslow strongly condemned the view that man's nature is evil. Man does have an inner core that he brings with himself at birth which (as far as we know) is definitely not evil, but is either what we call in our culture 'good' or else it is neutral. Maslow believed that a proof of man's goodness is that 'uncovering' therapy decreases aggression, hostility, greed, and other negative characteristics and increases love, kindness, and creativity. He concluded that the latter are deeper, more natural, and more basic characteristics than the former. The views of Rogers and the early views of Fromm coincide with those of Maslow in believing that man is basically good.

Freud, according to Staub, believed that man–woman is basically selfish. Staub's analysis emphasizes this aspect of Freud's views; others attach great significance to Freud's view of man as an aggressive creature.[2] Freud's

---

1. Staub, Erwin (1980). The Nature and Study of Human Personality. *Personality: Basic Aspects and Current Research*, ed. E. Staub, p. 23. Englewood Cliffs, N.J.: Prentice Hall.

2. Dilman, Ilham (1983). *Freud and Human Nature*, pp. 130–154. Oxford: Basil Blackwell. McAdams, Dan P. (1990). *The Person*, p. 56.

insistence on the primacy of Thanatos reflects his belief expressed in his dictum, "Homo homini lupus"—man is a wolf to man.[3] The views of Konrad Lorenz, who has had a profound influence on psychologists, are akin to those of Freud.[4] He told Richard Evans that he, Lorenz, considers aggression to be an integral part of human nature, manifesting itself spontaneously. "I'm convinced of it, I cannot prove it in man."[5]

Rollo May, in an open letter to Rogers entitled "The problem of evil"[6] contrasted his views with those of Rogers. He quotes Rogers:

> So I see members of the human species. . . as essentially constructive in their fundamental nature, but damaged by their experience.

To which May replies:

> But the problem of evil is so crucial that it is imperative that we see it clearly.

May then elaborates:

> I am pleading for a realistic approach to human evil. A colleague tells me that when you had your discussion with Martin Buber in Michigan you said, 'Man is basically good' and Buber answered, 'Man is basically good–and evil.'

San Diego: Harcourt Brace Jovanovich. Almost all textbooks describing Freud's theory of personality perceive him as viewing the person as aggressive.

3. Freud, Sigmund (1930/1961). *Civilization and its Discontents*, pp. 110–111. London: Hogarth Press.

4. Kimble, Charles E. (1990). *Social Psychology*, p. 467. Dubuque, IA: William C. Brown.

5. Evans, Richard I. (1974). A Conversation with Konrad Lorenz, *Psychology Today*, vol. 8:83–93.

6. May, Rollo (1982). The Problem of Evil: An Open Letter to Carl Rogers. *Journal of Humanistic Psychology* 22:10–21.

Social psychologists do not address the question whether man–woman is basically good or evil. They do, however, study aggression and related topics very extensively. It can be argued that if aggression is innate, then there is a basis to contend that man is not basically good or even neutral. This premise is strengthened if it is held, as Freud did, that aggressive energy must not be bottled up in the individual, for doing so strengthens it and leads to illness. In a recent text,[7] Aronson, Wilson, and Akert cite many studies involving animals and conclude that although aggression does not need to be learned, this does not however prove that it is instinctive. To draw the conclusion that aggression is instinctive, there must be physiological evidence of a spontaneous stimulation for fighting that arises from within the body alone. Some feel that such evidence exists.[8] Others contend that although aggressiveness exists and has evolved due to its survival value, nearly all organisms also seem to have developed inhibitory mechanisms enabling them to suppress aggression.[9] The authors then address the issue of human aggression:

> And where humans are concerned the social situation becomes even more important (Bandura, 1973; Lysak, Rule, & Dobbs, 1989; Baron & Richardson, 1992; Berkowitz, 1968, 1993). As Berkowitz (1993) has suggested, we human beings seem to have an inborn tendency to respond to certain provocative stimuli by striking out against the perpetrator. Whether or not the aggressive action is actually expressed is a function of a complex interplay between those innate propensities, a variety of learned inhibitory responses, and the pre-

---

7. Aronson, Elliot, Wilson, Timothy D., and Akert, Robin M. (1997). *Social Psychology*, 2nd ed., pp. 439–440. New York: Longman.
    8. Lorenz quoted in Aronson et al. Note 7, p. 439.
    9. Lare and Schultz quoted in Aronson et al. Note 7, p. 439.

cise nature of the social situation. . . much evidence
supports the contention held by most social psychologists that, for humankind, innate patterns of behavior are infinitely modifiable and flexible. This is illustrated by the fact that human cultures vary widely in
their degree of aggressiveness.[10]

The question whether true altruism exists is also relevant to our discussion. If it can be shown that there are
altruistic people, it would indicate that, at least for some,
basic goodness is a fact. Much research has been carried
out in an attempt to determine whether true altruism exists, and at present opinions are divided on this issue.
Aronson, Wilson, and Akert summarize:[11]

> The Toi and Batson (1982) study suggests that true al-
> truism exists when people experience empathy toward
> the suffering of another. But as illustrated by our ex-
> ample of Abraham Lincoln and the pigs, it can be ex-
> ceedingly difficult to disentangle people's exact motives
> when they help someone, and a lively debate over the
> empathy–altruism hypothesis has arisen. . . . Some
> researchers question whether people who experience
> empathy help purely out of concern for the person in
> need or, like Abe Lincoln, help in order to lower their
> own distress at seeing someone they care about suf-
> fer. The purity of our motives when we help others is
> a fascinating question that social psychologists con-
> tinue to address.

Social psychologists have directed their research efforts in the areas of aggression and altruism to ascertaining how people will act under differing conditions.
Aronson, Wilson, and Akert's statement regarding the

---

10. See note 7, pp. 439–440.
11. Ibid, pp. 409–410.

state of research in altruism is true for aggression as well. They write:[12]

> ... in short, to predict how helpful someone will be, it is most useful to know a lot about his or her personality and the nature of the situation he or she is in. Several studies have demonstrated that certain kinds of people are more likely to help in one situation, whereas other kinds of people are more likely to help in different situations.

Psychological science is not now in a position to offer a definitive answer to the question whether people are basically good or evil. There are major figures in psychology on both sides of the issue, joining long lists of illustrious thinkers throughout the ages who have wrestled with this problem. Experimentalists working in the fields of personality and social psychology are attempting to clarify some aspects by defining the social situations and delineating the parameters of personality makeup having a bearing on the question.

---

12. Ibid, p. 414.

THE JEWISH VIEW

The presentation of the Jewish position on the question of whether man is intrinsically good or evil focuses on how Judaism construes personality structure. It also addresses some of the factors which influence behavior. This approach is consonant with that of the social psychologists who stress the importance of situational conditions in directing behavior.

Discussion and analysis of the Judaic position by scholars usually begin by citing the verse:

> I will not again curse the ground anymore for man's sake, for the imagination of man's heart is evil from his youth (Genesis 8:21—Hertz edition of the Pentateuch).

In his commentary, Chief Rabbi Hertz of Great Britain notes:

> imagination. The Evil Inclination in man, *yetzer hara*, which too often gains the mastery over the Good Inclination, *yetzer hatov*.

Rashi, the greatest medieval Jewish commentator on the Torah, notes that the verse reads "from his youth." The Hebrew rendering of this passage hints, and this is how the sages understand it, that the *yetzer hara* is present in man from birth. This and similar passages, as well as rabbinic sources,[13] seem to postulate that human

---

13. Dessler, Eliyuhu E. (1964). *Michtav M'Eliyuhu* vol. 3, p. 361. Bnai Brak: Vaad Lekitvai Horav Dessler.

Hirsch, Samson R. (19th century/1955). *Yesodot Hachinuch* vol. 1, pp. 152-158. Tel Aviv: Netzach.

Solomon, Andy (1973). "Eros–Thanatos: A Modification of Freudian Instinct Theory in the Light of Torah Teachings." *Tradition* 14:90–101.

nature is, even if not entirely so, basically evil. This is how these sources are interpreted by John Hick, an outstanding contemporary scholar of comparative religion.[14]

Two approaches have been followed in dealing with the implications of this passage. Hirsch focuses on the term *yetzer,* interpreting it to mean an idea or goal created by the individual, not a driving motivational force.[15] Spero elaborates on this and suggests that *yetzer* "be equated with the individual himself." His argument, in part, is based upon talmudic sources assigning positive characteristics to the *yetzer.* Actually his reasoning constitutes a second approach, the gist of which can be comprehended and appreciated in the following quotation:[16]

> Thus, with regard to the classical situation of temptation, we would not speak of man as being torn between two conflicting desires—good and evil—but rather as being torn between a desire which is an expression of his character and a higher obligation which is a more true expression of his essential self—a conflict between what one feels he needs to make of himself and what he ought to be.

Spero's argument is designed to show (a) that the *yetzer hara* is not to be equated with the Freudian concept of Thanatos; (b) that the Judaic concept of human nature is not congruent with theories viewing human character as composed of large doses of evil.

Spero, Moshe H. (1975). "Thanatos, Id, and Evil Impulses," *Tradition* 15:97–111.

———— (1980). *Judaism and Psychology: Halakhic Perspectives,* Chapter 5. New York: Ktav Publishing House, Yeshiva University Press.

These writers discuss the issue quoting rabbinic sources. Citing them is not meant to imply that they feel that man is basically evil.

14. Hick, John (1989). *An Interpretation of Religion,* p. 32. New Haven: Yale University Press.

15. Hirsch, See Note 13.

16. Spero, Note 13, p. 80.

The structure of personality as envisioned by Judaism, presented in the following pages, places the question of goodness–badness of human nature in a different perspective. Defining and describing the cognitive, emotional, and volitional structural makeup of a person will demonstrate that the question as posed cannot be answered by either a flat yes or no. One must first specify which aspect of the person is being scrutinized, and only after this is clarified can a decision be reached as to whether man–woman is good or evil. Firstly, the question of the definition of *yetzer hara* will be addressed. The approach advocated incorporates aspects of Rabbi Hirsch's and Spero's understanding of the Jewish view of human nature, but, taken in its broadest aspects, constitutes a different view and interpretation of the term *yetzer hara*— evil inclination.

Perusal of classical Judaic ethical literature leaves no doubt that the concept of an evil inclination is an integral part of Jewish ethical philosophy. Rabbi Bachya Ibn Pakuda (twelfth century), *Hovat Halevovot*, Chapter 5; Rabbi Yonah of Gerona (thirteenth century), *Shaarai Teshuva, shaar rishon* paragraphs 1, 4, 10; Maharal M'Prague (sixteenth century), *Netivot Olam, netiv koach hayetzer*, Rabbi M. C. Luzatto (seventeenth century), and *Mesillat Yeshorim*, Chapter 2 all assign a central role to the evil inclination and its influence on human behavior. They sketch its parameters in detail and advise how to avoid and not succumb to its blandishments. They are just a few of the many moralists who expressed similar views.

There are two schools of thought as to its composition, its substance summarized by Rabbi Yisroel Salanter (Lipkin) in his influential "Mussar Epistle":[17]

---

17. Salanter, Yisroel, Nineteenth century/1944. *Mussar Epistle* trans. Hazedek, Student Organization of the Rabbi Isaac Elchonon Theological Seminary, Yeshiva University, and modified by author. New York: Hazedek Y.U.

One widely held opinion is that the evil inclination is
an impure force in man which entices him to sin, and
the good inclination is a sanctifying force which leads
him to goodness. This is the majority opinion of the
great scholars. Another opinion is that the evil inclination is man's lust. . .and the good inclination is
man's intellect which views the future in terms of divine reward and punishment. . . .It is clearly evident
that both opinions are correct. . . .

Rabbi Salanter arrives at this conclusion, that both
opinions are correct, after careful analysis of human motivation and behavior. He notes that people vary in their
mode of sinning, some being addicted to one sort of transgression, others to another. He concludes that this is due
to different temperaments. This explanation, he argues,
does not suffice. People are also driven to sin to enhance
their fame and bolster their egos; the desire for fame does
not, however, bring them to perform good deeds, despite
the fact that fame can be attained by following the righteous path. According to Rabbi Salanter, this can be explained if we posit the existence of pure and impure forces
which influence people.[18]

Having established that Jewish ethicists subscribe to
the concept of an evil inclination and having briefly considered its composition, the nature and direction of this
force bear clarification.[19] This, of course, is linked to the

---

18. Ibid.

19. The Ramban (Nahmanides), medieval Talmudist and bible
commentator second only to Rashi, writes in his preface to his commentary on Job that Satan is an angel created to entice people to do
evil. The Talmud (*Baba Batra*, 16:a) states that the evil inclination,
Satan, and the angel of death are one and the same, a clear indica-
tion that the *yetzer hara* is a spiritual force. Rabbi Hayim of Volozhin
writes in his classic *Nefesh Hachayim* (Chapter 6) that prior to Adam's
sin, the *yetzer hara* was not an integral part of Adam; this changed
with Adam's sin. Israel's acceptance of the Torah on Mt. Sinai brought

discussion above regarding the schools of thought as to its substance. The fact that Thanatos in the Freudian scheme is perceived as providing the energy and force for destructive action emphasizes the importance of clarifying this point. Maharal M'Prague (*Netivot Olam, netiv koach hayetzer*, Chapter 1) informs us that scripture and the sages portray the evil inclination as having two components: one identified with corporeality—lustfulness in the sexual sense—the other a spiritual force whose operational sphere is the spirit, the soul—enticing the person to idolatry. This division should be understood as prototypical, the lustful encompassing all bodily material lusts, the other including all transgressions of a spiritual nature.[20] In Chapter 4, he focuses on their similarities, emphasizing that both estrange man from the Almighty. His reasoning and approach are more meaningful if the division into two components is viewed as representing the two conceptions of the evil inclination discussed above. The Maharal explicitly states (Chapter 4) that the *yetzer hara* and the *yetzer hatov* are autonomous forces motivating man's behavior. In another of his writings (Chidushai Agadot, Baba Batra, p. 16A), he comments on the relation between Satan, the angel of death, and the *yetzer hara*. He regards them as separate and distinct entities which coalesce in a spiritual sense.

The thesis that the Maharal's partitioning of the *yetzer hara* be considered prototypical is supported and further refined by the Gra's (Rabbi Eliyuhu, the Vilna Gaon, eigh-

---

about a reversal to the state of affairs existing prior to the sin. Unfortunately, the sin of the golden calf caused a second reversal.

20. Other scholars as well view the *yetzer hara* in this fashion, see: Rabbi Isaac Chaver, p. 43. *Maalot Hatorah* 1880/1987. Jerusalem: Keter Hatorah. See also Rabbi Zadok of Lublin (nineteenth century/1951), *Takanot Hashovim*, p. 45. Bnai Brak: Yahadut Publishing Co., and his *Yisroel Kedoshim*, p. 57. New York: Saphrograph Co. The latter is a famous Hassidic master.

teenth century) thinking on the subject. In at least three places in his commentaries on scripture (Genesis 4:23; Proverbs 1:11; Job 5:2), he describes the evil inclination as composed of two parts: (a) a lustful inclination, alluded to in the seventh commandment prohibiting adultery; (b) an inclination to anger and aggression, alluded to in the sixth commandment prohibiting murder.

POSITIVE ATTRIBUTES OF THE *YETZER HARA*—THE EVIL INCLINATION

Spero's analysis of the concept of *yetzer hara* has been mentioned. He quotes a *midrash* (comments by the sages on scripture quoted in the talmud or in other writings are referred to as midrash, Genesis Raba 9:9).

> ... 'and behold it was good' is a reference to the yetzer, while 'behold it was very good' is a reference to the evil yetzer. But, is the evil yetzer to be considered very good? Yes, for without the evil yetzer man would not marry, built a house, beget children, or engage in business.

The idea expressed in this midrash is woven by the Gra into an explanation of the *mishnaic dictum* (Talmud, Berachot, 54A) that one is obligated to serve the Almighty with both inclinations, the *yetzer hatov* and the *yetzer hara*. He prefaces his explanation by stating that the reason for the creation of the *yetzer hara* is not merely or solely that man–woman resist its blandishments and thereby be rewarded. On the contrary, the *yetzer hara* is indispensable, it motivates behavior. Without the *yetzer hara* life is not possible. How, then, is the *yetzer hara* considered a vessel with which to serve the Creator? That, when satisfying one's physical needs, the sole motivation should be heeding the Creator's wishes, not the indulgement of one's desire.[21] The Gra elaborates on this concept adding an additional dimension to its meaning:

> The reward in the coming world is earned and based upon transforming the bitter to sweet. This is the secret of the yetzer hara which was instilled in man so

---

21. Rabbi Eliyuhu of Vilna (Eighteenth century/1986). *Orot Hagra* p. 74. Bnai Brak: Kollel Tel-Ganim.

that he could transform it to good. Something which
is good from its inception is 'good,' but the term 'very
good' is reserved for that which was evil and was
turned into good.[22]

This concept is further proof that the evil inclination—
evil, is part of the human personality. However, this fact
is, in reality, a blessing because it creates the condition,
it affords the opportunity, for man–woman to transform
evil into good. The ability to do so is uniquely human—
angels cannot do so—and, in a very real sense, is the reason for man's–woman's creation. There are kabbalists and
Torah scholars who maintain that evil does not exist. It
is with us only because it leads to good and should be
viewed as evil only in a figurative sense. On a deeper level
it is good.[23]

---

22. Rabbi Chaver, *Maalot Hatorah*, p. 58, writes that, were it not
for the *yetzer hara*, man–woman would be an angel with no choice
but to do good. This is not praiseworthy. Perfection is attained by
transmuting all blemished traits into worthy ones.

23. M'Halinov Rabbi Shmuel, Nineteenth centry/1985. *Minhat
Shmuel* p. 26. Jerusalem: Kema. This thesis is discussed and held by
many Torah scholars. Minhat Shmuel is singled out and quoted because the author, who is associated with the Gra's school, states
clearly and explicitly that, even in this world, evil is a metaphorical
appellation. Others write of evil as being nonexistent in other more
sublime worlds.

COMPARISON AND EVALUATION OF THE
PSYCHOLOGICAL AND RELIGIOUS POSITIONS

Freud revised his theory of personality following World War I, at which time he promulgated "Thanatos", the death–aggression force. This led psychologists and others to see him as a leading exponent of the position that man–woman is intrinsically aggressive, aggression leading them to behave malevolently to such a degree that humans are to be regarded as basically evil. Lorenz, cited above, supports a similar notion. A comparison between this position and that of the Jewish thinkers is called for. They seem similar. Freud speaks of Eros and Thanatos, while Jewish moralists view lust and aggression as the components of the *yetzer hara*. Spero's argument, noted previously, that Thanatos is not be equated with the evil inclination is logical and compelling.[24] Hirsch and Spero both argue that human nature is basically good (i.e., this is presented as the Jewish position) or, at the least, neutral. They base their contention on many sources. (For example, Hirsch cites the prayer recited every morning, "the soul you have implanted in me is pure.") Their argument, in large measure, rests upon the novel interpretation of the term *yetzer* as discussed above.

The author agrees with Hirsch's and Spero's assessment of human nature as being basically good. However, the writer maintains that Jewish scholars throughout the ages viewed and interpreted *yetzer hara* as an evil inclination. This is so even if, as has been demonstrated, the *yetzer hara* has positive redeeming features. This obligates us to show how it can nevertheless be held that Judaism regards man as basically good. It will be argued and demonstrated that the *yetzer hara*, despite its power, impor-

---

24. Spero, Moshe H. See Note 13.

tance, and influence does not represent the totality of the person and does not characterize his/her personality. The discussion will proceed to elaborate on the theological basis of the Jewish perception of human nature. This analysis will, hopefully, clarify the unique Jewish formulation of personality structure and shed light on the issues with which this chapter deals.

STRUCTURE OF PERSONALITY

Genesis (2:7) teaches us that the human body was created from the earth, infused with a soul and became a living creature. A clear division exists between body and soul. Whereas there aren't any conceptual difficulties regarding the body, the soul, being of divine origin, is a complex entity having a number of components.[25] The fusion of body and soul is problematic from a theological point of view. What is the nature of this fusion? Does a new entity emerge? The material body is devoid of feeling and intellect. The soul is divine. Man is a combination of both. But what does this mean? Are both components, body and soul, of equal importance and power? Or does one take precedence over the other? What is the nature of their interrelationship? Who and what is man–woman? The Gra,[26] drawing upon kabbalistic sources, identifies the result of the fusion as an entity which is the repository of feelings and senses, the being which eventually will stand in judgment and be rewarded or punished—the *ruach*. The *ruach* is the part of the person having and exercising freedom of choice to do good or evil. It is the uniquely human component of man–woman. It is distinct from the soul, the *neshama*, which is divine in the sense that it can be considered a segment of the Creator. The *neshama* is not an integral part of the person or an attached appendage, but hovers, in a spiritual sense, above him/her. The body, inert, lifeless, begins to function when the *neshama* and *ruach* become attached to it by way of an entity called *nefesh*. This is the word used in Genesis 2:7 describing the creation of man, "and the person became a living

---

25. The kabbalists list three major components of the divine *neshama*: (a) *chaya*; (b) *yechida*; (c) *neshama*. The term *neshama* also denotes the entity composed of the above three parts. See, for example, Rabbi Hayim of Volozhin (note #19), *Nefesh Hachayim*, the first gate.

26. Gra, Rabbi Eliyuhu of Vilna (1976). *M'Pairushai Hagra Al Hatorah*, p. 61. Jerusalem: Tinnitz.

nefesh." The end result is like a chain, the divine *neshama* linked to the uniquely human component of man–woman, the *ruach* which, in turn, is linked to the *nefesh*, the living counterpart of the material body. Death is defined as the severance of *ruach* from body. Reward and punishment are administered by rejoining them (Talmud, Sanhedrin, 91B). This was the response of Rebbi, the compiler of the Mishna, to a question posed to him by the Roman Emperor Antoninus.

This conception of the structure of personality is extended and elaborated upon by the Gra's principal disciple, Rabbi Hayim of Volozhin, in his writings "Nefesh Hachayim" and "Ruach Hayim." In Chapter 3 of Ruach Hayim he writes that the body, the material self, is intrinsically inclined to sin. In spite of this bodily tendency, a person can choose to lead an exemplary life and thereby transmute the body into a spiritual entity. Conversely, sinning taints the *ruach,* causing it to lose its spirituality. In the fifth chapter, he discusses the concept of evil and the power it wields.[27] The force was created so that

---

27. The writings of Rabbi Shneur Zalman (late Eighteenth and early Nineteenth centuries), the founder of *habad hasidus* (Lubavitch), are in some respects similar to the ideas expressed by the Gra and his discicple Rabbi Hayim of Volozhin. In his most important work, *Tanya*, he describes personality structure as being composed of *nefesh, neshama, ruach*, etc. In Chapter 29, he deduces from the prayer recited every morning "the soul (*neshama*) that you have implanted in me is pure" that the soul, the *neshama* is not the person. The person is the receptacle, the recipient of the divine *neshama.* This reasoning seems to undermine Rabbi Hirsch's contention that man is good, a contention based upon his understanding the prayer as meaning that man is the *neshama*, or becomes one with the *neshama.* Rabbi Shneur Zalman's keen analysis teaches us that the *neshama* is not the person. There are exceptions; the fully righteous can reach a spiritual level or pinnacle where "*person*" and divine *neshama* are one and the same. However, this state of affairs is so rare that it can be disregarded for the purpose of this analysis. Adam, prior to his sinning, was in this category of holiness. See Rabbi Meir Simcha (1978). *Meschech Chochma*, p. 26. Israel: Mifalai Seforim.

humans, the pinnacle of creation, can subjugate it, causing it to disintegrate. This is the purpose of creation, to acknowledge God and actively fight and conquer the evil that resists this acknowledgment. This conflict is a spiritual one. Rabbi Hayim sees this force as active only in our material world. It is not of any consequence, does not exert any influence, in a sense does not exist in other spiritual worlds. This concept does not leave room for rebellion by Satan, by evil, as envisioned by John Milton in his epic poem *Paradise Lost*. Even Satan, in the Jewish view, is an instrument of God's will.

The following portrait of human character emerges. The essence of man–woman is not evil. He/she, the 'I', is perceived as subject to opposing pressures. The *yetzer hara*, the evil inclination, advises the person to lead a lustful, aggressive life. The *yetzer hatov*, the good inclination, exhorts and attempts to persuade the person to lead a just and righteous existence. The *yetzer hatov* is identified as emanating from the *neshama*.

There is another point which bears considering. This concerns the power that the inclinations—good and evil—have at their disposal. Are they equally powerful, or is one more powerful than the other? Rabbi Hayim, quoted above, writes that the body's natural inclination is to sin. This would seem to tip the balance of power in favor of the *yetzer hara*. Indeed, in the fourth chapter of *Ruach Hayim* he states that the evil inclination is more skilled and labors more industriously at his calling than does the *yetzer hatov*. He believes that the Almighty granted him this power, for were it not so, the *I*, the *person,* would not be tempted by the *yetzer hara* to swerve from the righteous path. The divine *neshama's* influence is so pervasive and compelling that the person would gravitate toward the good. This reasoning is based upon a theological axiom. The world needs to be structured in a way that ensures the freedom to choose between good and evil. This is possible only if the *yetzer hara* is enabled to counteract the naturally powerful influence of the *neshama.*

To summarize, the *I*, the *person*, is "good" due to the enveloping embrace of the divine *neshama.*[28] The Creator, however, has endowed the evil inclination with the necessary power to ensure that the person will always be confronted with situations in which freedom of choice is equally balanced.[29] From this perspective, the Jewish concept of personality, specifically whether man is good or evil, is a sophisticated one. Man is basically good. However, since reward and punishment are justifiable only if complete freedom of choice is predicated, it must follow that the *yetzer hara* be powerful enough to balance the person's natural tendency to goodness. This conception is vastly different from the Freudian or Lorenzian views, which consider the person to be lustful and/or aggressive. It also differs theoretically from Buber's perception of man as being both good and evil, although, operationally, it is similar to Buber's formulation.

The Freudian and Lorenzian position is based upon the conception of the person in materialistic terms. Judaism, as well, views the bodily aspects of the human as veering toward improper behavior; however, the body is only one component of the complex human entity. It is not the deciding, choosing element of the person, of the "I". The Judaic and social psychologists' positions are similar in their attention to a host of factors impinging on the

---

28. The "elder of Kelm," Rabbi Simcha Zisel Ziv, stresses the goodness of man. He depicts the person as brimming with goodness far exceeding his/her evil. See Simcha Z. Ziv, Nineteenth century/ 1980. *Kitvai Hasaba M'Kelm,* p. 48. Bnai Brak: Siftai Chachomim.

29. See Rabbi Eliyuhu E. Dessler's discussion of this principle (1964). *Michtav M'Eliyuhu,* vol. 2, p. 238; vol. 3, p. 184. Bnai Brak: Comm. for Publication of Rabbi Dessler's writings. See also his discussion of *nefesh, ruach,* and *neshama* in the fifth volume, 1996, p. 385.

decision-making process of the person. They are dissimilar in that, for Judaism, the complexity is rooted in its perception of personality as a many-layered entity, whereas social psychology stresses, almost exclusively, extraneous factors.

3

The Unconscious

DEFINITION AND BRIEF HISTORY

The school of psychology rooted in Freud's teachings and, to a lesser degree, other schools such as the Jungian and Sullivanian, are known as dynamic psychologies. Their systems stress the dynamic interplay of the powerful psychic forces that shape personality and determine behavior. The interplay involves unconscious motivations unknown to the person and/or repressed by him/her. They are viewed as stemming from recesses deeply embedded in the personality, hence the term depth psychology. Since the early part of this century, this way of thinking about people has exerted a powerful and pervasive influence on modern society and culture. Almost all branches of knowledge and aesthetics have been influenced by psychoanalytic and depth psychology's insights. Suffice it to say that it is not exaggerated to claim that the twentieth century has, in no small measure, been directed and shaped by the writings of Freud and other kindred souls. This includes the field of ethics as well, which will be addressed in a later chapter. A crucial component of depth psychology is the concept of the unconscious. The emphasis on the unconscious served to lessen the importance of the cognitive and rational aspects of personality, thereby changing our perception of human personality.

The concept of the unconscious did not originate with Freud.[1] However, he, more than others, mapped its borders and described its methods. He traced its fluctuations and the routes it travels, its mode of operation as it goes about its business of influencing behavior.[2] Kendler[3] describes the unconscious clearly and succinctly:

> The unconscious portion of a person's mind is that of which he is unaware of, but which nevertheless can influence his behavior. One of Freud's major assumptions is that all drives, conflicts and experiences may affect our behavior even though we are unaware of their influence.

1. Whyte, Lancelot L. (1960). *The Unconscious Before Freud.* New York: Basic Books.

2. Ellenberger, Henri F. (1970). *The Discovery of the Unconscious,* pp. 474–550. New York: Basic Books.

3. Kendler, Howard H. (1974). *Basic Psychology,* p. 531. Menlo Park, CA: W. A. Benjamin Inc.

METHODOLOGY USED IN ASCERTAINING THE JUDAIC VIEW

Addressing the question of how Judaism views the concept of the unconscious raises the issue of how, by what methods, can the Jewish view be arrived at and formulated. Judaism is not essentially a philosophical or psychological system or theory. It does not use their language and terms, and its tenets are not presented in a systematic orderly fashion. The Bible is not a theological treatise in the usual sense of the word. The very word Torah means teaching; it instructs people which path to follow, it teaches a way of life, a code of behavior, it is not a philosophical discourse or a series of lectures on emotional stability. Its commandments, *mitzvot*, cover all aspects of human behavior, and relate to all aspects of human personality. Some govern relations between people, having for their basis logical principles. Other *chukim*, are *mitzvot* which humans cannot comprehend or discern the reasons for observing.[4] The tales recounted in scripture and rabbinical writings are an integral part of those works. The lives of the great and others depicted are a rich and invaluable repository of wisdom and ethical principles. The sages interpreted both the laws and the stories in the *mishna, talmud,* and *midrash.* Their teachings comprise the oral law that Judaism holds to have been given to Moses on Mt. Sinai together with the written Torah.[5] The oral law, which, at a later date, was codified and permitted to be recorded, encompasses legal discussions and

---

4. See the sixth chapter of Maimonides (Rambam) introduction to *Pirkai Avot* ("The Sayings of the Fathers," a tractate of the *Mishna* and Babylonian Talmud); Rashi (the foremost medieval Jewish commentator on scripture and Talmud), Leviticus 18, 4: 18, 9: and Nahmanides (Ramban) comments on these verses.

5. See Rashi's explanation and comments on the first verse of Chapter 21 in the Book of Exodus.

aggadic (homiletic passages) teachings. The latter is the main vehicle chosen by the sages to teach and transmit ethical moral values. It is also a conduit for imparting philosophical, theological, and kabbalistic principles. To further this purpose, it was purposely couched in ambiguous and abstruse language.[6] The above points to the obstacles faced when attempting to arrive at a definitive opinion as to what is the Judaic position on a philosophical or psychological question. Add to the above the fact that healthy controversy is found on every page of the Talmud, reflecting opposing viewpoints. In addition, the scholars and rabbis following the codification and final editing of the talmud were often divided as to which talmudic opinion is binding. Notwithstanding these difficulties, the proper methodology is to research the literature following accepted talmudic principles and reasoning, to sift and filter alternatives toward reaching a decision or opinion consonant with other accepted decisions. Psychological principles can be deduced from both *halakhic* injunctions and *aggadic* parables.[7] This method should be employed to determine whether the concept of the unconscious is compatible with Judaism.

Some scholars have not fully exhausted the possibilities inherent in this method and have concluded that the

---

6. Rabainu Shlomo ben Avrohom Aderet (Rashba), (1991). *Chidushai Horashba, Pairushai Hoagodot,* p. 3. Jerusalem: Mosad Horav Kook. The Rashba, one of the foremost Talmudical scholars of the Middle Ages, was the leading authority of his age in Spain. See also Rabbi Moshe Chaim Luzatto, *Yalkut Yediot, Maamar Al Agodot* (Israel, Publishing house and date not given). This author, known as Ramchal, lived in the seventeenth century in Italy and emigrated to Israel, where he died. His works have been published many times. A leading kabalist and ethicist, he is highly revered and respected, his name a household word amongst scholars.

7. Rabbi Maier Bar-Ilan began to systematically analyze *halakhic* literature to understand the psychological principles involved. See his essay "*Halchot Hameusodot Al Techunot Hanefesh,*" in *Azkoroh,* ed. Yehuda L. Fishman, 3:4, pp. 209–220. Jerusalem: Mosad Horav Kook.

concept of the unconscious is inimical to Judaic thought. Amsel[8] rightfully assumes that a cardinal principle of Judaism is that people be held accountable and responsible for their behavior. Any concept that undermines this is foreign to Judaism. He also assumes, erroneously so, that to attribute behavior to unconscious motivation is to espouse a deterministic position tantamount to stating that people cannot be held responsible for their actions. This leads him to declare that the concept of the unconscious is in direct opposition to the Jewish view. Klein also believes that Freud's determinism leads to a negation of the principle that a person is responsible for his/her behavior.[9] This is so, Klein reasons, because the person is directed, in Freud's view, by a conglomerate of forces, many of which lay hidden from the person within deep layers of the unconscious. Klein writes "one begins with an explanation of human behavior and ends with an excuse for it."

This argument links the issue of the unconscious to the issue of free will. Free will is of interest far beyond the uniquely Jewish features of the problem, involving general theology and other disciplines as well, such as jurisprudence and criminology. The need or wish to see a person as a free entity from a psychological point of view has already been discussed by many writers and there is no need to repeat the arguments.[10] There are, however, other points pertinent to the arguments advanced by Amsel and Klein which should be examined.

----

8. Amsel, Avrohom, *Judaism and Psychology*, pp. 144–164. New York: Feldheim.

9. Klein, Joel (1979). *Psychology Encounters Judaism*, p. 7. New York: Philosophical Library.

10. For example: Chein, Isidor (1972). *The Science of Behavior and the Image of Man* (New York: Basic Books); and Higgins, John W. (1959). "Psychiatry and Religion," in *American Handbook of Psychiatry*, ed. Silvano Arieti, vol. 2, pp. 1783–1788. New York: Basic Books. These are classical representations of the issues. In recent years much has been written on the issue.

It is assumed by the writers that, in Freudian theory, the instinctual forces, due to their unconscious nature, are more powerful than the forces of rationality and, therefore, will always emerge victorious in any confrontation with the ego. This is a questionable interpretation of Freudian theory. Gill points out that repressive forces as well as instinctual forces can be unconscious.[11] Delegating repressive forces to the unconscious invests them with the same properties possessed by the instinctual forces. This undermines the supposition that adherence to the concept of unconscious motivation means allegiance to the deterministic position.[12]

Careful reading of the writings of theorists who reject the unconscious because they view it as opposed to Jewish teachings reveals that for some there is no clear distinction between the concept of the unconscious and the Freudian image of man–woman. For them, accepting the concept of the unconscious is synonymous with accepting what Freud held to be the content matter of the unconscious; the sexual and aggressive drives. This is a false assumption; theoretically, the concept of the uncon-

---

11. Gill, Merton M. (1963). "Topography and Systems in Psychoanalytic Theory," *Psychological Issues* 3:2,260–288.

12. Klein, *Psychology Encounters Judiasm*, p. 57, realizes that invoking the principle of free choice invariably leads to the position that other theories, for example, reinforcement theory, which emphasizes the function of rewards in strengthening habits, and mechanistic theories, which maintain that responses are triggered by stimuli, must also be viewed as not being in the spirit of Torah. Amsel, however, seems to wholeheartedly embrace the behavioristic position. This exposes him to the same critique he levelled at the concept of the unconscious. In stating, as he does, that a person is capable of overcoming the second nature acquired by habit, he does not resolve the dilemma. It is unethical to hold an individual accountable if the individual is not accorded equal opportunity to choose between opposing courses of action. See also Spero's critique of Klein. Moshe H. Spero (1979). "Critique of, On the Conflict Between Applied Psychology and Judaism," *Journal of Psychology and Judaism* 4:1:32–48.

scious can be accepted while at the same time rejecting Freud's instinctual theory. The two issues are separate and exclusive, a point overlooked by many.

Freud's views on the unconscious underwent considerable transition in the course of his lifetime. A major revision occurred in 1923, when Freud abandoned his topographic system of conscious, preconscious, and unconscious in favor of the structural system of id, ego, and superego. The concept of the unconscious, as it pertains to the relationship of mental concepts to consciousness, remained in the new system. The theory of the instincts was also revised in his later years, when "Thanatos," the death or aggressive instinct, was elevated to a status equal to, if not greater than "eros." Other psychoanalytic schools parted with Freud on the issue of the contents of the unconscious. Arguments advanced for or against the validity of the theory of the instincts cannot be used for either the legitimization or refutation of the concept of the unconscious. In sum, one can believe that unconscious forces exert a powerful influence on the person and direct the individual's behavior, and yet differ with Freud or other dynamic psychoanalysts as to what these forces are.

Some voice their objections to accepting the unconscious because they feel that doing so means peeling away the positive aspects engendered by the sense of guilt. In their view, the psychoanalytic approach serves to excuse behavior and does away with a sense of guilt. It is true that some psychologists seem to object to guilt feelings, and therapists have been known to have overstepped their mandate and exhorted their patients to do away with all guilt feelings. This is not a new issue and Mowrer's denunciation of this trend is well known.[13] Later chapters

---

13. Mowrer, Orval H. (1950). *The Problem of Anxiety in Learning Theory and Personality*, pp. 531–561. New York: Ronald. This is the first of many articles and books by Mowrer on this subject. A par-

will deal with the contemporary emphasis on subjectivity, its relation to egotistic values, and its concomitant rejection of accepting responsibility.[14] These, unfortunately, not uncommon aberrations do not represent the essence of dynamic psychology and should not be used as a rationale for the acceptance or non-acceptance of the concept of the unconscious.

The assumption by some thinkers that psychoanalytic theory stresses instinct expression may be responsible for their belief that dynamic psychology scoffs at guilt feelings. This, however, is not an accurate understanding of dynamic psychology. The Freudian approach does indeed hold that overrepression of the instincts can lead to pathology, but this is not the full picture. Sublimating the instincts, even in classical theory, is a positive defense mechanism upon which civilization is based. Society's standards are not necessarily regarded as arbitrary and guilt is not merely an artificial artifact to be dispensed with.

---

ticularly interesting presentation of his views is in his essay (1972), "On the Delights and Consequences of Conscience Killing," in *Conscience, Contract and Social Reality,* ed. Ronald C. Johnson, Paul R. Dokecki, and Orval H. Mowrer, pp. 25–34. New York: Holt, Rinehart & Wilson.

14. See Gertrude Himmelfarb's essay (1997), "Revolution in the Library." *American Scholar* (New York: Spring 1997, reprinted in the *Key Reporter,* vol. 62, no. 3, Spring (1997). She writes "The mainspring of post modernism is a radical—an absolute, one might say—relativism, skepticism, and subjectivism that rejects not only the idea of greatness, but the very idea of truth."

THE UNCONSCIOUS: JEWISH SOURCES

It should not be surprising to find that the concept of the unconscious is not foreign to Judaism; on the contrary, it finds in it a receptive and comfortable niche. The concept of the unconscious is simple to comprehend, but possesses depth—a combination which forges it into a powerful tool. Jewish tradition views scripture and rabbinical literature in similar fashion—on one level, simple; and on other levels, deep. A text which is easily comprehended by a child contains knowledge that can be teased out only by great scholars. The same texts are pored over by scholars of great intellectual prowess who cull new knowledge and insights, a process repeated and ongoing over three thousand years.

In direct contrast to arguments which identify the concept of the unconscious with a forgiving attitude to sin, Friedman claims that the concept broadens the parameters of responsibility for sin. His analysis uncovers areas where psychoanalytic theory can be fruitfully used to "enhance our appreciation of a substantial portion of the commandments of the Torah."[15] The sacrificial laws are cited as an example, specifically the sacrifice (*chatos*), which is obligatory when one has sinned. This sacrifice is required only when the transgression is committed unknowingly, and only then can the sacrifice be considered a propitiation. Certainly, he contends, this shows that one is responsible for one's actions, even when the sin is committed unwittingly, without prior intent. This law's meaning is enhanced if one accepts the contention that unconscious forces influence an individual's behavior.

---

15. Friedman, Moshe (1974). "Freudian psychoanalysis and its Relation to the Jewish Concept of Sin," *The Jewish Parent* 27:1:14–17.

Rabbis Ginzberg[16] and Weinberg[17] consider the concept of the unconscious to be consonant with Judaic
thought. Moreover, they claim that Rabbi Yisroel Salanter
(Lipkin), the founder of the Mussar Movement in the
middle and late nineteenth century, predated Freud as to
the emphasis and use of the unconscious. Their thesis is
that Rabbi Salanter described the unconscious and fully
realized its implications before Freud. Writing of "inner"
forces whose influence on behavior is more potent than
conscious "outer" forces, Rabbi Salanter pictured these
forces as having qualities associated with the dynamic unconscious. They can be repressed, but burst forth with
unprecedented power in times of stress when intellectual
forces are dormant.

Rabbi Salanter introduced the concept known to us
as the unconscious by relating a hypothetical story. A
scholar and pious man has an apt student to whom he is
strongly attached and a son, a wastrel whom he despises.
They all reside in the same town and are asleep when a
fire breaks out. The scholar is awakened from a deep sleep
and informed that both his son and student are in danger. The scholar will instinctively hasten to his son's res-
cue because, being half asleep and not in full possession
of his rational cognitive powers, the instinctual "inner"
forces are dominant over the rational "outer" forces.

The concept is used to explain two apparently contradictory *aggadic* sayings. The patriarch Abraham is described in one story as eagerly and joyously obeying God's
injunction to sacrifice his son Isaac, while in the other
he is depicted as weeping. Rabbi Salanter resolves this

---

16. Ginzberg, Yehuda L. (1947). "*Shnai Horim Gedolim,*" *Talpiot,*
Third year, vol. 1:2:35–42.
17. Weinberg, Yechiel Y. (1969). "*Al Hachidush Hamadai Shel
Torat Hamussar.*" *Seredai Aish,* vol. 4, pp. 333–334. Jerusalem: Mosad
Horav Kook.

contradiction by invoking the concept of inner (unconscious) forces and outer (conscious) forces. Abraham, on
a conscious level, cheerfully prepared himself to carry out
God's wish, but his inner instinctual forces caused his
weeping. Abraham's greatness is that the powerful inner
forces did not deter him from cheerfully doing what he
considered his duty. They, however, could not be denied
their measure of grief. The inner unconscious components
cannot be completely eliminated or controlled to the extent that they will not be experienced or felt. The person,
however, has the ability to behave according to his/her
rational dictates and prevent his/her inner forces from dic-
tating his/her overt behavior.

The inner forces are also called by him "unclear"
forces as opposed to the outer, "clear" forces. His intention is to focus on the fact that he considers the inner
forces, by virtue of their unclear nature, unknown to the
individual. This, to him, explains the roots of their power.
They are not present in the person's consciousness, consequently they seem to come from nowhere and overpower
the unwary.

This analysis deals with the unconscious as the relation of mental concepts to the unconscious. The theory
of the instincts or any other theory concerning the contents of the unconscious is not germane to the central
issue. Rabbi Salanter's very behavior is an example of his
perception of the power and influence it has. He was wont
to examine his doodlings, claiming the contents of his unconscious were thus revealed to him.[18]

The concepts did not remain in the realm of the purely
theoretical, but were developed and incorporated in the
system he developed. Since a person may be motivated
by forces of whose existence he/she may be unaware, and

---

18. Katz, Dov, (1964). *Tenuat Hamussar*, vol. 1, 5th ed., p. 251.
Jerusalem: Brody Katz.

which lie outside the cognitive rational sphere, it follows that the intellect may not be powerful enough to cope with them. The emotions must be marshalled and molded into an effective tool and, thereby, strengthen the rational forces. The methodology employed to effect this transformation and to forge an effective instrument is Rabbi Salanter's unique contribution to the study of ethics. He introduced the following methods:

(a) the study of ethical texts, *mussar*, is to be conducted at a slow rate in loud, mournful tones;

(b) phrases that have touched the reader or, for whatever reason, are deemed relevant, are to be repeated as many times as is necessary to affect the self;

(c) a special house of study for this purpose is to be set aside exclusively for mussar learning.

The above methods are designed to facilitate the attainment of the goal, transforming the conscious, rational, ethical concepts into unconscious affective forces. This will endow them with greater power to influence behavior. Whereas psychoanalysis wishes to make the unconscious conscious, the Mussar movement's methodology stresses transmuting conscious ideals into unconscious forces.

The first two methods described above are rooted in psychological principles; the third seems to be in the nature of a technical or practical necessity. The methodology utilizing the first two innovations have withstood the test of time, whereas the third has not. *Yeshivot*, the institutions where the intense study of Talmud is pursued, have, by and large, adopted his approach. The study of *mussar* is, in those yeshivot cast in the Lithuanian mold, an accomplished fact. Houses dedicated exclusively to *mussar* study have not taken root.

The explanation presented above, linking Rabbi Salanter's contribution to the study of ethics with his deep understanding of the workings of the unconscious, is not the one offered by his disciple Rabbi Blazer. The latter, himself a world famous Talmudist, edited Rabbi Salanter's letters and *mussar* essays. The above and Rabbi Blazer's mussar writings, together with a brief biography of his teacher, comprise *Or Yisroel*, the first major source book for the Mussar movement. Rabbi Blazer tells us that his teacher, Reb Yisroel (Salanter), taught that the study of ethics has two functions: (a) the acquisition of factual knowledge, defining what is to be considered ethical; and (b) the transmutation of one's moral ethical principles into moral behavior. The first function, mastery of the relevant factual knowledge, comes about as a result of diligent study in precisely the same way that Talmudic proficiency is acquired. However, and this is the crux of Reb Yisroel's innovation, assimilating these principles, transforming them so that they form an integral part of the personality and are thus able to influence and guide behavior, requires a different method. This technique is rooted in emotion, as Reb Yisroel explicitly states in many of his writings. Reb Yisroel, in his famous *Mussar Epistle* (*Iggeret Hamussar*), asserts that undisciplined, unfettered imagination leads man to blindly follow the dictates of desire, unmindful of reason and oblivious to possible negative consequences. This state of affairs must be altered, but how? Are reason, intellect, powerful enough to withstand the onslaught of undisciplined imagination which can and does distort truth and reality? At this point, Rabbi Salanter's unique approach manifests itself. Reason can and must be shielded from imagination's unfettered and detrimental influence by enveloping it with a protective coating, as it were, of powerful emotional affective forces. Henceforth, ethical literature is to be studied not only for knowledge of its content, but for its emotional impact as well. Rabbi Salanter, in Essay #30 (*Or Yisroel*), delegates to the intellect the task of researching, uncovering, and defining the parameters of wisdom. The task of affect is to penetrate the heart, overcoming its obstinancy, allowing it to be impregnated with reason. In modern terminology, this can be called existential knowledge, it "is participating knowledge, not detached objective knowledge; and it involves a practical or existential commitment to its object." [19]

Reb Yisroel's theoretical basis and technique can be understood by relating it to the dynamic interplay between forces of the intellect, imagination, and emotions as described above. However, tying the approach and technique to his understanding of the unconscious,[20] as has been demonstrated, endows it with richness and sophistication and buttresses its theoretical basis. The potential ability of every trait and attitude to be transformed into a powerful inner force is the cornerstone of his technique. Most individuals are well aware of what constitutes moral attitudes and behavior. The difficulty lies in convincing the heart to follow the intellect, the body to heed wisdom's dictates. He reasoned that only by transforming the basic personality makeup, by embedding the proper norms in the person's unconscious, can he/she hope to follow his/her conscience and obey the call of moral standards. Although he does not make direct mention of the unconscious in his *Mussar Epistle*, he alludes to the same inner forces in relation to *mussar* study in one of his letters.[21]

---

19. This phrase was coined by Randall based upon religious existentialism. See Randall, John H., Jr. (1958). *The Role of Knowledge in Western Religion*, p. 94. Boston: Starr King Press.

20. Rabbi Yisroel Salanter's understanding of the intricacies of the unconscious is described in Hillel Goldberg's *Israel Salanter: Text, Structure, Idea* (New York: Ktav, 1982).

21. Reb Yisroel Salanter (Lipkin) (1989). "Sixth Letter," in *Or Yisroel Hasholaim*, ed. Rabbi Yitzhok Blazer, pp. 71–81. Bnai Brak.

IMPLICATIONS OF THE INNER-OUTER FORCES CONCEPT

Rabbi Salanter's concept of inner-outer forces led him to consider implications of his model. The following example demonstrates how the concept may be developed to show that a person's personality composition is complex and intricate.[22] He postulates that the division between inner-outer can theoretically bring about a situation such that, for a given individual, one part of him/her may be moral, and the other immoral. This is so because a person's inner traits are a function of education. A person reared and educated by parents who themselves were ethical and stressed morality will be a moral ethical person insofar as the outer forces are concerned. However, the inner forces may be immoral if this was the given at birth and was not properly attended to. The opposite situation is also possible. If a person was not fortunate enough to have been reared by ethical God fearing parents in an ethical environment, in all probability the outer forces will not urge the person to lead a moral life and will prevail, in spite of the fact that the person may have been granted inner moral character traits. This explains why a moral person, under stress, may act and eventually become immoral. The reason for this change is that the person's inner traits, despite a proper education, remained immoral because the education focused only on outer traits and not on the inner forces. Similarly, an overtly immoral person may become a moral ethical individual if the inner forces were basically good and the person, for some reason, was inspired and decided to alter his/her behavior. In both instances, the inner forces gained ascendancy over the outer forces.

---

22. ——— *"Maamar Beinyan Chizuk Lomdai Torotainu Hakedosha,"* pp. 295–305.

Reb Yisroel Salanter applies his thesis to better understand the character of Yerovom ben Nevat, Israel's first king. Yerovom rebelled against Rechavom, Solomon's son, splitting off Israel from Judah. The sages inform us (tractate Sanhedrin 101b) that Yerovom merited the monarchy and was granted it by God for performing a meritorious deed. This was his rebuke of Solomon some years before. The *Midrash Rabah* (*shemini*, Chapter 12), however, regards his act as disrespectful of King Solomon. At first glance, it seems that the Midrash contradicts the Talmud. Rabbi Salanter interprets them so that they complement one another. He cites sources showing that Yerovom's outer forces were of the highest quality; his scholarship was without blemish. However, this was not the case pertaining to his inner forces. They were riddled with very grave flaws. His rebuke of King Solomon, which entailed a degree of personal danger, was in order. He was not obliged to do so due to the danger involved; nevertheless, he disregarded the danger. This, however, can be considered a noble and worthy act only if he, himself, is faultless. Only then can his rebuke of King Solomon be considered an act of great courage and piety. Having established that his inner traits were severely flawed, his act of rebuke was disrespectful and caused the Almighty to test him by granting him power and observing how he would act. His action on one level was praiseworthy and merited reward; on another level, it was hypocritical. Had he looked deeply into his own psyche he would have realized that he was tainted, by the very traits for which he rebuked the king. He was rewarded for the good he did and punished for the very same act because his motives were not pure. His punishment was his being exposed to power and its perils. He was given the kingship, but in wielding power, his evil inner traits overcame his finer outer traits. The very same intensity and conviction that led him to disregard personal danger and rebuke King Solomon, in a sense, caused his downfall, clouding his judgment in such a way that he failed to minutely examine the purity of his inner motives.

This penetrating and sophisticated analysis is an excellent illustration of Rabbi Salanter's deep and profound understanding of behavior. It also shows the usefulness of the concepts he taught. Rabbi Salanter taught that the person is a many-layered entity; consequently his/her innermost being is unchartered territory. He is quoted as saying "a person lives with oneself for seventy years and nevertheless does not recognize himself." [23] The following chapter will examine how his concepts can be utilized in interpreting scripture.

Rabbi Blazer, the editor and compiler of Reb Yisroel's letters and other books, used the concept to illustrate the complexity of common everyday behavior.[24] A person who hurts a friend or acquaintance turns to the friend, admits the wrongdoing, and asks to be forgiven. The friend, as often happens, makes light of the incident and doesn't wish to continue the conversation. It seems that the hurt party is acting magnanimously. Rabbi Blazer raises the possibility that the injured person does not wish to hear an apology and forgive. He/she may prefer that the other remain unforgiven and, therefore, indebted to the injured person.

A novel interpretation of a Talmudic teaching, incorporating a basic axiom of dynamic psychology, is made by Rabbi Dessler, a leading luminary of the Mussar movement.[25] The Talmud (*Megillah* 3a) states that, although the

---

23. *Tenuot Hamussar*, p. 301.

24. Blazer, Yitzhok (1974). *Kochvai Or*, p. 255. Jerusalem: Rabbi Blazer did not use the terms, inner–outer, clear–unclear forces. This point is discussed by the author in his article (1981), "*Lebirur Musag Habilti-Muda Betnuat Hamussar.*" *Samuel Belkin Memorial Volume*, ed. Moshe Carmilly and Hayim Leaf, pp. 36–42. New York: Yeshiva University.

25. Dessler, Eliyuhu E. (1983). *Michtav M'Eliyhu*, Vol. 4, p. 298. Jerusalem: Vaad Hafozat Kitvai Hagra Dessler.

person may not see or know (referring to Chapter 10, Book of Daniel, where it is related that when Daniel saw a vision, others did not, but were nevertheless frightened), the person's *mazal* does see or know. Rabbi Dessler interprets *mazal*, in this context, to mean subconscious or unconscious. The sages' teaching is that, although a person may know, he or she unconsciously may choose to repress that which part of the person does not wish to know. The repressing agent or reason is, according to Rabbi Dessler, a manifestation of the constant inner struggle between good and evil. This, of course, goes beyond dynamic psychology, but the dynamics are similar to the teachings of depth psychology, a person's inner needs repress something he or she really knows.[26]

The Talmud (*Nedarim* 81a) teaches that the reason for the temple's destruction was unknown to the wise men and prophets of that generation. Even the angels could not fathom why. The enigma was finally resolved by the Almighty. Rabbi Chasman[27] deduces that a person is capable of delving deeply into the depths of his/her psyche to learn things so complex and deep, they are unknown even to angels. Not only is the person capable, but he/

---

26. The works of the Hasidic masters also demonstrate psychological acumen in their discussions, parables, and interpretations. Although Hasidic literature does not contain a systematic analysis of the unconscious comparable to Rabbi Salanter's, one can readily discern that some of the masters were familiar with the concept. The *Sefat Emet* (Torah, Book of Numbers, Matot) speaks of the thoughts a person has of which he is not aware, using this concept to explain Joshua's behavior. The sages criticize him for waging unnecessarily prolonged wars. They attribute this to Joshua's realization that the cessation of the wars liberating Canaan would mean that his own demise was imminent. The *Sefat Emet* stresses that prolonging the war was not done consciously. However, on the unconscious level, this seemed to have somehow influenced him. This led to postponement of the liberation of Canaan.

27. Chasman, Yehuda L. (1973). *Or Yohail.* Vol. 2, 4th ed., p. 139. Jerusalem: Peer.

she is obliged to do so, for, were it not so, why was the temple destroyed? Can a reason which is not capable of being known be deemed sufficient justification for the razing of the temple? Obviously, this is an impossibility. The logical conclusion is, and the Talmud teaches, that a person is capable of reaching deeply into the unconscious and utilizing the knowledge found there to modify behavior. This holds true, even for matters of the greatest complexity and depth.

DISSIMILARAITIES BETWEEN THE CONCEPTS: MODES OF THINKING

A clear distinction was made between the concept of the unconscious and the contents or substance that psychoanalytic theory views as being in the unconscious. It was argued that acceptance of the concept of the unconscious does not necessarily imply accepting psychoanalytic theory as to its substance. To better understand the connection forged in Freudian psychoanalytic theory between the unconscious and instinct theory, it is worthwhile to analyze the mental processes of the unconscious. Rapaport[28] quotes Freud:

> In the psychology which is founded on psychoanalysis we have accustomed ourselves to take as our starting point the unconscious mental processes, with the peculiarities of which we have become acquainted through analysis. These we consider to be the older primary processes, the residues of a phase of development in which they were the only kind of mental processes. The soverign tendency obeyed by these primary processes is easy of recognition; it is called the pleasure–pain (lust-unlust) principle, or more shortly the pleasure–principle. These processes strive towards gaining pleasure; from any operation which might arouse unpleasantness (pain), mental activity draws back (repression).

A concise description of the mechanics of the primary process is given by Ford and Urban.[29]

---

28. Rapaport, David (1951). *Organization and Pathology of Thought* (p. 317). New York: Columbia University Press.

29. Ford, Donald H., and Urban, Hugh B. (1964). *Systems of Psychotherapy*, p. 139. New York: John Wiley & Sons.

Primary process thought does not follow the rules of
formal logic; it is unreflective; its temporal relationships
and sequences are disorderly; it tends to be imagistic
rather than verbal, though not entirely; contradictory
ideas and images may exist together; separate ideas
tend to fuse into one (condensation); and changes in
relationships among images or verbal thoughts readily
occur, such as reversal of figure–ground relationships.
Such thought is generally organized around experiences or aims related to psychological energies or responses (instinctual drives). Dreams exemplify such
thought.

We learn that primary process thinking, a primitive
version of thought, is governed by the pleasure principle,
a primitive tendency. This connection is made and emphasized in Allport's description and analysis of this facet
of Freudian theory.[30]

Let us look more closely at the terms primary and secondary process. Freud's choice of these terms betrays
his whole theory of the nature of man. What is instinctual, blindly self-centered, immediately demanding,
largely unconscious is primary. What is rational, controlled, adult is secondary. To be sure, the terms have
also an innocent flavor of time: the infant's primary
demand for gratification is earlier than all secondary
rational developments. But Freud means more than
this. Not even an adult escapes the primacy of the
primacy process in his life. Freud insists that "the ego
has no energy of its own. It does not exist until energy is diverted from the id to sustain the secondary
processes that constitute the ego."

---

30. Allport, Gordon W. (1961). *Pattern and Growth in Personality*
p. 148. New York: Holt, Rinehart & Winston.

These quotations present a clear picture of the thought processes operative in the unconscious. They also demonstrate how, in the Freudian framework, the primary thought process is inexorably linked to instinct theory.

One searches Rabbi Salanter's writings in vain for an analogous description of the thought processes of the inner forces. He differentiates between what he terms universal forces, defined as emotions or personality traits present in every person, and non-universal forces, defined as emotions or traits not present in all, found in only a segment of humanity.[31] In his sixth letter to his students, he explains why the inner forces are more powerful than the outer forces and are more influential in directing and charting an individual's behavior. He attributes this to the dormancy of the inner forces, the consequence of which is a lack of discernment by the individual of the forces' presence. Their dormancy is a function of their being deeply embedded in the psyche; they are part and parcel of the person—there is no need for them to constantly impinge their presence on the person's consciousness. There is no mention in Rabbi Salanter's writings of differing thought processes by which to discriminate between the inner and outer forces, be they universal or non-universal.

The different approaches in the perception of the unconscious stem from different theoretical conceptions of the relation between conscious and unconscious. The Freudian model places the unconscious in the id; consequently, it is subservient to the whim of the pleasure principle. The pleasure principle functions by means of primary process thinking, unreflective and illogical. These thought processes are the residue of a previous phase of

---

31. See Note 22.

development, although they operate in the present as well. This is not the case in the model advanced by Rabbi Salanter. The inner forces are not linked to a structure of personality comparable to the id of the Freudian framework.[32] There is, therefore, no need to postulate a unique mode of thinking specific to these forces. These forces are powerful because they have become an integral part of the individual's personality, so deeply embedded that they qualify to be considered as inner forces.

The model proposed by Rabbi Yisroel Salanter can be accommodated with what, at first glance, seems to be a different, contrasting approach. *Sefer Hachinuch* is a four-teenth century classic which summarizes the *mitzvot* (laws) covered in each weekly reading of the Torah on the Sabbath. The author repeatedly emphasizes the value of the act of performing mitzvot. This is so, he writes, because it is axiomatic that overt behavior shapes inner personality. The importance attached to the unconscious seems to be in opposition to the *Sefer Hachinuch*'s reasoning. However, Rabbi Salanter's unique formulation of the unconscious as unclear inner forces allows us to embrace the concept of the unconscious and nevertheless accept the principle that "outer influences inner." Inner does not imply that an idea, trait, or attitude is rooted in and can stem only from the depths, but rather that the idea, trait, or attitude is now firmly and deeply embedded in the psyche. This aim can be achieved by stressing the idea, trait, or attitude and tying it to affect, thereby inserting it deeply in personality. It has already been noted that this is the cornerstone on which Rabbi Salanter's program for learning mussar is based. This argument can be advanced to narrow the chasm between behavioristic theory, predicated on the same principle as that propounded by the

---

32. Nor are they to be perceived as the evil inclination as has been proposed. See Aaron Rabinowitz, note no. 24.

Sefer Hachinuch, with the concept of the unconscious as formulated by Rabbi Salanter. Unconscious forces are more powerful than conscious forces; nevertheless, the unconscious itself can be shaped by conscious effort employing behavioristic methodology.

Rabbi Salanter did not, as has been noted, develop a theory of primary process thinking. He does not, therefore, mention in this writing distortions of thought processes associated with abnormal behavior. This does not mean that he didn't realize that thought processes can be distorted. It means that the concept of the primary process as a phenomenon beginning at birth and continuing to wield great influence in adulthood is not present in his thinking. Thorough reading of his essays, especially essays 29 and 30, as well as the *Mussar Epistle*, reveals that, in contrast to Freud, he held the noncompromised intellect in the highest esteem.[33] This is in the classical Jewish tradition as exemplified by Maimonides and Rabbi Bahyah Ibn Pakuda in his ethical treatise *"Duties of the Heart."*

---

33. See *Or Yisroel Hasholaim*, note no. 21.

DISSIMILARITIES RELATING TO THE CONTENT OF THE UNCONSCIOUS

The content matter of the psychodynamic unconscious is associated with instinct theory which is rooted in biology. Rabbi Salanter did not view biological drives, needs, or instincts as constituting the content of the inner forces. He believes, as has been noted above, that forces (inner or outer) can be perceived as belonging to one of two clusters, universal or nonuniversal. He attributes great importance to this division; a person is capable of mastering a nonuniversal force, but cannot completely master a universal force. He also says that a nonuniversal force can be biological; it follows that a biological force can be mastered. In essay #30,[34] he lists three factors which explain why people's personalities differ: (a) biology, meaning genetic inheritance; (b) social influence; (c) the individual's efforts. He does not indicate anywhere that any one factor is more important than another. This line of reasoning is receptive to the contemporary emphasis on sociological and social factors as important shapers of personality and directors of behavior.[35]

The fact that Rabbi Salanter was not constrained to theorizing within the confines of a biological frame of reference has another important consequence. Allport writes that many psychologists feel that Freud's position emphasizes the animalistic aspects of human nature.[36] Fromm, articulating humanistic psychology's critique of Freud, takes Freud to task for excluding other needs from his

---

34. Ibid., essay #30.

35. Hall, Calvin S., and Lindzey, Gardner (1957). *Theories of Personality*, p. 115. New York: John Wiley & Sons.

36. Allport (note 30) agrees with Jung that it doesn't necessarily follow from the premise that since emotional difficulties are rooted in the unconscious, the unconscious harbors only what is evil, dirty, and dangerous. Rabbi Salanter would concur. P. 148.

basic theoretical foundation, regulating them to offshoots of the sublimating process. For the humanistic school of psychology, other needs which "stem from the condition of his existence, the human situation" are no less basic.[37] In contrast to Freud, Reb Yisroel (Salanter), not being confined to biology, was able to think in other directions; consequently, he was able to hold that the universality of a force is not dependent upon the biological factor. He also saw no difficulty in believing that whether a force is inner or outer is not biologically determined; neither is it dependent upon its being a universal force. It need only be deeply embedded to qualify as being inner and, as shown above, it is not tied to a particular structure of personality. In this system, all tendencies and needs possess the potential to become inner. He also taught that inner forces can include needs which may be, as he calls them, of a "meritorious nature."[38]

---

37. Fromm, Erich (1955). *The Same Society*, p. 28. New York: Rinehart. See also exchange of letters between Freud and Binswanger (1955) pertinent to this issue, in *Psychoanalysis and Existential Philosophy*, ed. Hendrik M. Ruitenbeek, pp. xviii–xix. New York: E. P. Dutton & Co.

38. See Note 34.

DISSIMILARITIES: DARWINISM

The linkage of Freudian theory and biology demonstrates the influence of Darwinism on psychoanalysis. Biological science in the latter half of the nineteenth century was heavily influenced by Darwinian biology. Murphy[39] maintains that "the influence of Darwinism upon psychology during the last quarter of the nineteenth century probably did as much as any single factor to shape the science as it exists today." Ellenberger[40] outlines the influence of Darwinism on Freud's thinking:

> Like so many of his contemporaries, Freud was an enthusiastic reader of Darwin, and the influence of Darwinism on psychoanalysis is manifold. First, Freud followed Darwin in the shaping of a psychology based on the biological concept of the instincts. . . Second, Freud followed Darwin in his genetic outlook on the manifestations of life, . . . Third, Freud seems to have transposed to psychology and anthropology Haeckel's 'law of recapitulation'; the principle that 'ontogeny recapitulates phylogeny' finds its equivalent in Freud's assumption that man's individual development goes through the same phases as the evolution of the human species, and that the Oedipus complex is the individual's revival of the murder of the old father by his sons. Finally, Darwin's influence can be recognized in Freud's elaboration of a biological theory on the origin of human society and morals, taking as a starting point the consideration of an early, hypothetical ancestor of man who lived in small groups or hordes.

The constantly growing importance of Darwinistic theory consolidated the influence of biology on psychol-

---

39. Murphy, Gardner (1949). *Historical Introduction to Modern Psychology*, p. 116. New York: Harcourt, Brace.
40. *The Discovery of the Unconscious.*

ogy. A negative consequence is that it led to insufficient consideration of the effect of social factors on psychology. The influence of Darwinism led to other developments in psychology and eventually to exerting profound influence on the course of human history. Allport writes:[41]

> We are emerging from an epoch of extreme irrationalism when human motivation has been equated with blind will (Schopenhauer), with the struggle for survival (Darwin), with instincts (McDougall and others), with the steam boiler of the id (Freud). Under the powerful influence of these doctrines, the role of the 'intellect' has been considered negligible.

Allport's statement deepens our understanding of Freud's emphasis on the role of the drives or instincts, and his almost total exclusion of the role of the ego. Freud not only saw himself as a scientist following the biological and physical models, but was no doubt also influenced by Darwin's doctrine of the struggle for survival which, according to Allport, downgrades the role of the intellect. It seems superfluous to note that Rabbi Salanter's writings do not reflect the above.

Darwinism was not confined to biology: it reached out to cast its spell on other disciplines as well. Ellenberger[42] writes that "the most important influence of Darwinism was felt through Social Darwinism, that is, the indiscriminate application of the concepts of 'struggle for life,' 'survival of the fittest,' and 'elimination of the unfit' to the facts and problems of human societies."

He supports his opinion by citing a list of injustices perpetrated in the name of Social Darwinism, for example:

---

41. *Pattern and Growth in Personality*
42. *The Discovery of the Unconscious.*

Militarists throughout the world turned it into a scientific argument for the necessity of war and for maintaining armies. The pseudo-Darwinian philosophy that persuaded the European elite that war is a biological necessity and an inescapable law has been held responsible for the unleashing of World War I. A long series of politicians proclaimed the same principle, culminating with Hitler who repeatedly invoked Darwin.

The unconscious of Freudian theory, predicated on biology and drawing from Darwinism, inevitably leads to its perception as a repository of hedonistic and aggressive instincts. Rabbi Salanter's concept of inner forces is similar to the Freudian unconscious only in that it has the dynamic characteristics that the unconscious has. The characteristics of the unconscious which stem from its being conceived in a biological framework are conspicuously absent from the inner forces of Salanterian theory.

The deprecation of religion by Freud is also traceable to the influence that biology, and specifically Darwinian biology, exerted in shaping Freud's thinking. His views on religion are well known; an excellent summary and critique are provided by Ostow.[43] Freud tied religion to the psychic life of the child and the neurotic. He elaborated on this idea and maintained that God is the object of the individual's projected love, hatred, and guilt feelings. He is the likeness of one's father and, in reality, nothing other than an exalted father. Religious feelings achieve profundity because they represent a return, in adult life, to infantile feelings of awe. The child, in real life, foregoes the love and protection of the father and in his stead assumes

---

43. Ostow, Mortimer (1959). "Religion: Contributions From Related Fields," in *American Handbook of Psychiatry*, vol. 2, ed. Silvano Arieti, pp. 1789–1801. New York: Basic Books.

to have a supernatural father. The centrality of the Oedipal conflict and its resolution, involving repression and its effect on the unconscious, figures prominently in the Freudian analysis of the origins of religion.

Much has been written concerning Freud's analysis of religion.[44] The point made here is that Freud's perception and acceptance of Darwinian biology, including perhaps the principles later known as Social Darwinism, channeled his thinking and led him to write as he did about religion. This is similar to his blind adherence to nineteenth century physics. His homeostatic theory, based upon the supposition that there is only a fixed amount of energy available to the individual, which must be accounted for, is an offshoot of nineteenth century physics. Physics has, of course, advanced, leaving Freud anchored to an outdated system. It is, therefore, not surprising that aspects of his theory based upon that system are no longer viewed favorably even by his followers. In similar fashion, his reliance on the then-accepted but now outmoded biological theory has shackled his theory to untenable positions.[45]

Matarazzo's assessment of the state of psychoanalysis' contributions to western thought serves to focus attention on salient features of the issues discussed:[46]

The many important contributions of psychoanalysis (e.g., the role of unconscious factors in human behav-

---

44. Rieff, Philip (1979). *Freud: The Mind of the Moralist*, 3rd ed. Chicago: The University of Chicago Press. See also: Gresser, Moshe (1994). *Dual Allegiance*, pp. 154–225. New York: State University of New York Press.

45. Sulloway, Frank J. (1992). *Freud: Biologist of the Mind*, pp. 257–276; 361–392. Cambridge: Harvard University Press.

46. Matarazzo, Joseph D. (1973). "The Practice of Psychotherapy is Art and Not Science," in *Creative Developments in Psychotherapy*, ed. Alvin R. Mahrer and Leonard Pearson, vol. 1, p. 365. New York: Jason Aronson.

ior and the vast richness and complexity of interpersonal phenomena) have been assimilated, quietly and imperceptibly, into many areas of Western intellectual life... Those aspects of psychoanalysis which did not survive close scrutiny, such as many aspects of symbolism and the exaggerated role of primary instincts in everyday behavior, have been downgraded to a position of rapidly diminishing influence.

The argument presented here is that those aspects of Freud's theory which relied almost exclusively on the physics and biology of his day have not stood the test of time and have been discarded, precisely as the theories upon which they were based have been disowned. This does not, however, explain why, according to Matarazzo, Freud's use of symbolism has fallen into disrepute. Perhaps, as others have said,[47] although Freud has relegated spiritual and aesthetic values to outcomes of sublimation, and has denigrated religion, in a sense he has created a new religion having its own trappings. This, in turn, has been criticized by other scientists who relate to that as Freud related to religion.

Rabbi Salanter's approach to the unconscious emphasizes those aspects which have withstood the test of time. It seems almost trite to point out that Freud was a psychiatrist; the nuclei of his opinions were formed and shaped by his daily contact with disturbed patients. It is, therefore, not surprising that he mistrusted the intellect, the ego, seeing as he did that a developed intellect did not ensure a healthy balanced emotional life.

---

47. Robinson, Lillian H. (1986). "Psychoanalysis and Religion: A Comparison," in *Psychiatry and Religion: Overlapping Concerns*, ed. Lillian H. Robinson, pp. 2–20. Washington, D.C.: American Psychiatric Press. Robinson quotes a number of theorists who maintain that psychoanalysis is not a science but a belief system. See also Wood, B. G. (1981). "The Religion of Psychoanalysis," *American Journal of Psychoanalysis* 40:13–22.

His theory has been challenged on clinical grounds. Even greater criticism has been directed at his attempt to apply his theory to understanding the development of civilization and to explaining all cultural manifestations as rooted in sublimated instinctual energy.[48]

---

48. *Pattern and Growth in Personality,* p. 150. n. 30. See also Abraham Maslow, *Toward a Psychology of Being,* p. 26 D. Van Nostrand: Princeton, N.J., 1962.

4

The Use of the Unconscious in Bible Interpretation

The thesis presented in the previous chapter was that the concept of the unconscious is not inimical to Jewish thought; on the contrary, it can deepen our understanding of certain concepts and facets of Judaism. This chapter examines that proposition. Rabbi Grodzinski, a leading scholar of the Mussar movement who perished in the Holocaust, affirms this in his writings. He expounds on the importance of understanding personality and human motivation in depth.[1]

> Without a proper understanding of the nuances of personality, its composition and complexity, one cannot hope to understand why the Torah saw fit to repeat its warnings and exhortations. One cannot begin to fathom the commandment (mitzvah) to walk in His ways. All the mitzvot which refer to the duties of the heart cannot be fully comprehended.

---

1. Grodzinski, Abraham (1978). *Torat Avrohom*, p. 191. Bnai-Brak: Kollel Avraichim Torat Avrohom.

Rabbi Grodzinski demonstrates in detail the truth of this statement. This chapter extends his approach to include the behavior of some biblical figures as an additional example of the potency and veracity of his thesis. Utilizing the insights gained through use of the concept of the unconscious enriches our understanding of their behavior. The premise that understanding the actions of people depicted in scripture necessitates probing deeply into their personality makeup is not foreign to the classical Jewish commentators. They were attuned to the language of the Bible, noting its complexity and realizing the significance of even minor variations the Torah uses when depicting events. Moreover, the acronym *pardes* is a well-known description of the conceptualization of Torah into four components: *peshat*—the obvious literal meaning; *remez*—interpretation based upon a hint embedded in the language; *drash*—interpretation arrived at by comparing the verse in question with other verses by traditional homiletic methods; *sod*—referring to the "deeper" meaning based upon Kabbalistic principles. This division is not meant to imply that each component is a complete and self-contained approach and that scholars have the option of choosing one over the other exclusively.[2] It should rather be understood as a means of attaining deeper understanding by projecting Torah as a multilayered body of knowledge and information with each layer necessary for a fuller understanding. This is so even when the interpretation arrived at by pursuing one method seems to contradict an interpretation arrived at by another.[3]

---

2. Talmud Bavli (Sanhedrin 34A) comments on the verse (Jeremiah 23:29), "As a hammer splits a rock," just as a hammer's blow causes many sparks, in like manner a verse can be interpreted many ways.

3. See Rashi (Numbers 6:9) "I therefore state, let's interpret and understand the verse in straightforward fashion (*peshat*) while concurrently accepting the '*derash*.' Moreover, the four layers are the basic

The Torah (Exodus 18:1–13) relates that when Moses told his father-in-law Jethro what had transpired in Egypt, the miracles and the punishment meted out to the Egyptians, Jethro rejoiced. However, the word used to describe Jethro's reaction is not the common term depicting joy. The term used is *vayichod* not *vayismach.* Rashi, the greatest medieval Jewish commentator, offers two meanings of the word *vayichod.* One is *peshat*—Jethro rejoiced; the other, *drash*—he was chagrined: literally, his flesh crept with horror on contemplating the fate of the Egyptians, a people with whom, according to the sages, he had, in the past, maintained close relations, serving as their advisor. It seems as if we are confronted with two contradictory interpretations. This, however, is not what Rashi wishes us to understand. Following the principle outlined above, it is to be understood as testifying or referring to two different aspects of human nature, both simultaneously present and in operation. The Torah is essentially relating to two different levels of Jethro's psyche. Each level expresses a different truth and reflects one part of the complex human personality.

This principle can be applied to the realm of *halakha* (Jewish law) as well. A child, when informed of a parent's death, is required to recite a blessing indicating acceptance of God's will and affirming his/her belief in the justness of God's decision. If the parent's estate is inherited by the child, an additional blessing is required acknowl-

---

ones. The sages teach us, "there are seventy faces to Torah." See Gra's (Rabbi Elijah of Vilna) commentary on Solomon's 'Song of Songs' 1:2. The 'Rim,' founder of the Gur Hasidic dynasty, is of the opinion that the four levels are concomitants of the four worlds discussed in Kabbalah (*Chidushai Horim Al Hatorah,* Note 21, p. 45). It is interesting to note that this approach to scripture interpretation, acceptance of the premise that different interpretations have validity, has been adopted by Christian theologians. Aquinas feels that this is an honorable testament to scripture. *Pocket Aquinas* (1960) ed. V. W. Burke, p. 317. New York: Pocket Books.

edging this and thanking Him for the good fortune.[4] Accepting the principle that humans are many-layered organisms, capable of having different and even opposing sentiments at the same time, explains what, at first glance, seems strange and contradictory. Expressing grief and acceptance of His will and judgment is a difficult task, requiring considerable emotional strength. This difficulty is compounded by the obligation to express thanks for the material benefits. Jewish teaching accepts the fact that the human spirit is capable of experiencing both sentiments simultaneously.

The concept of the unconscious, or inner, unclear "dormant" forces as Rabbi Salanter referred to them, was discussed in the previous chapter. It was shown how he used this concept to explain the biblical narrative depicting the near sacrifice of Isaac by his father, Abraham. Other examples were also presented. This chapter advances this train of thought by noting other examples where the concept of the unconscious proves to be a useful interpretive tool, enhancing our understanding of scripture.

Rabbi Salanter quotes a *midrash* which seemingly places Eliezer, Abraham's servant and disciple, on the same spiritual level as that of Abraham.[5] Rabbi Salanter expresses amazement that the sages seem to view Eliezer as the spiritual equal of the patriarch Abraham. In addition, the sages are critical of Eliezer for apparently wishing to marry off his daughter to Isaac, which the sages

---

4. Talmud, Berachot 5B.

5. The teachings of the sages in the Mishna or Talmud (oral law) are commonly referred to as *midrash* when espousing an ethical or moral point. The rabbis' usual method is to offer an interpretation of a story or single verse in the Bible. It also refers to a body of rabbinic literature such as *midrash rabah* or *midrash tanchuma* devoted primarily, though not exclusively, to moral teachings. The term *Aggadah* is frequently used when non-halakhic teachings or comments are the subject matter.

deem inappropriate. We are confronted with a paradox; on the one hand, Eliezer is roundly criticized; on the other hand, he seems to be held in the highest esteem, equal to that of Abraham. Rabbi Salanter's solution is based upon the principle that human behavior and motivation are complex and many layered. He postulates that there are two levels to be considered when describing conflict between good and evil inclinations, specifically when and if the good inclination has the upper hand. This can be a result of good overpowering evil or, on a higher level, transforming evil. Those who reach the first level act righteously and behave properly, but remain susceptible to evil, whereas those who have reached the pinnacle do not even desire to do evil. There is no difference on a behavioral level between the two classes; the distinction lies in the purity of their motives. Consequently, Eliezer was the equal of Abraham on a behavioral level—both refrained from doing evil and were not blemished in any way. However, Abraham purified himself to the extent that he had no desire to do evil; his evil inclination had been transformed into a force for good. This is in contrast to Eliezer who, although he had completely subdued his evil inclination, did not transmute it into good. At this level, the evil still exerts its influence—one's judgment cannot be completely trusted, in spite of the fact that the person does not succumb behaviorally to its blandishments.[6] This analysis recognizes the enormous influence wielded by forces embedded deeply in the person's psychological makeup, the unconscious. Even a towering spiritual personality cannot completely rely on his/her judgment and must recognize the possibility that unconscious powerful forces may influence one's judgment.

---

6. Salanter (Lifkin), Yisroel (1978). *Or Yisroel Hasholaim*, ed. Yitzchok Blazer. Bnai Brak: Essay no. 30. Also, *Kitvai Rabbi Yisroel Salanter*, ed. M. Pechter, pp. 134–135. Jerusalem: Mosad Bialik.

OTHER EXAMPLES

Rabbi Simcha Zisel Ziv was one of Rabbi Salanter's fore-most students. He followed in his mentor's footsteps and is known for his deep and incisive analyses of human behavior. This led him to found schools (*yeshivot*) with the express purpose of preparing promising young men to excel in both Talmudic studies and character in the spirit of his teacher Reb Yisroel. The leading luminaries of the Mussar movement (referring to the followers of Rabbi Salanter) in the late nineteenth and early twentieth centuries were either his or his students' pupils.

The midrash teaches that the Almighty seemed to accept the patriarch's Isaac's prayers to a greater extent than those of his wife Rebecca. The reason given by the midrash is that the prayers of a righteous person whose parents were also righteous have greater intrinsic value than those of a righteous person who is not the offspring of righteous parents. This midrash needs to be explained; reason would seem to dictate the opposite. Moreover, Rabbi Ziv quotes sources indicating that a righteous person living among evil people is more praiseworthy than one who lives in the company of other righteous individuals. Rabbi Simcha Zisel's analysis and explanation are an example of his profound understanding of human motivation.[7] He prefaces his explanation by quoting the sages, whom he understands as holding the opinion that the patriarchs were spiritual equals. They differed in their emphases and character, but were equally God fearing, spiritually pure, and exalted. This is so although Abraham had no one to learn from, whereas Isaac and Jacob were taught by their parents. He explains this by pointing out that known truths are more difficult to absorb and completely integrate into

---

7. Ziv, Simcha Z. (1964). *Chochma Umussar*, vol. 2, pp. 198–200. Jerusalem.

one's psyche and emotional makeup. This is so because one does not need to exert oneself, to direct all available energy to achieve the truth. It is there, it is within reach. If, however, the person is not content to rely only on tradition, on the given, and strives with all his/her energy to arrive at the truth, to understand it in depth, to be fully cognizant of its complexities and nuances, the task is even more formidable. One must start from scratch, from the beginning. There is no foil on which to sharpen one's perception; great effort must be invested to be able to do away with one's preconceptions and previous knowledge.[8] If the individual is not daunted and is unflagging in his/her devotion to achieve the truth, then the spiritual level attained by this person is even higher than that of the person who was not taught. This explains why Isaac's prayers are considered to be on a higher level than those of Rebecca. Although this example does not specifically

---

8. It seems that Rabbi Ziv is making the following point. There are two different aspects to be considered. Reward: It may well be that a person reared in a materialistic environment who resists its blandishments will be more highly rewarded than a person brought up in a spiritual environment. However, there is another aspect: spirituality. He presents the example of a person overcoming the flawed inborn traits that posed an obstacle to spirituality. This is an impressive achievement. However, one who was blessed with good character traits but did not rest on his laurels and elected to become more spiritual, in a sense was faced with a more difficult task than the first person. His inborn traits naturally channeled him to good, spirituality did not pose a challenge, but he had to overcome inertia. If he works at the task of becoming more spiritual and succeeds, his level of spirituality is higher than that of the first person. Rabbi Ziv's reasoning explains why each patriarch followed a different path, one not chosen by the others, in his search towards truth. Abraham chose *chesed* or loving-kindness; Isaac, *gevurah* or spiritual strength; Jacob, the path of *emet* or truth. Each realized that merely following in the others' footsteps would be the hallmark of superficiality. Each accepted what was taught to him by father or grandfather, but Isaac and Jacob chose new ways so that their understanding of God's relation to humans would be broadened and deepened.

relate to the unconscious, its emphasis on depth and its attention to the intricacies of the psyche demonstrate the workings of emotional forces akin to those operating when the unconscious is invoked. The ability to free oneself from preconceptions and given knowledge is dependent upon freeing oneself from unconscious factors which tend to oppose the decision to begin fresh.

Rabbi Yeruchem Levovitz, a disciple of Rabbi Ziv, explains a puzzling aspect of Jacob's behavior.[9] The sages criticize him for concealing his daughter Dina in a closed box when the reunion between him and his brother Esau took place (Genesis, 33). This act is not mentioned in the text, but the sages deduce that this took place based on their minute reading of the text. They explain Jacob's behavior as stemming from his concern that Dina's beauty would entice Esau to ask for her hand in marriage. This act was viewed by the sages as being responsible for Dina's abduction by Shechem as related in Chapter 34. Jacob, they teach, was punished for not allowing a possible marriage between Esau and Dina, which may have led to Esau's reformation. Dina's beauty, fine character, and gentleness may have had a good influence on her uncle. Jacob's opposition to this possible union is not viewed with favor by the sages. Rabbi Levovitz quotes his teacher Rabbi Ziv as expressing astonishment at this criticism. The sages, in many of their writings, depict Esau as evil—a murderer and idolater. In the light of this judgement, should Jacob have been a party to a possible marriage between his daughter and such a person? There is no question but that, on the very slight chance that Dina may influence Esau, such a marriage cannot be condoned. Halakha does not sanction such a union and there cannot be a moral obligation to initiate such a move. How,

---

9. Levovitz, Yeruchem (1967). *Daat Chochma Umussar,* vol. 1, p. 262. New York.

then, are we to understand the sages' harsh criticism of Jacob? Rabbi Ziv, quoted by his disciple, explained the sages' criticism as directed toward Jacob's manner, of concealing Dina in the container. He rather picturesquely describes Jacob slamming the container door shut, not simply closing it. This shows that Jacob's decision, although correct, was flawed in the decision-making process. His actions were not completely purely motivated. Unknown even to him, it was contaminated by personal considerations. He was not guided solely by halakhic or moral considerations. This was considered by the sages as a sin. Jacob's high moral stature obligates him to be purely motivated and not to allow even a minor personal consideration to be part of the decision-making process. This same act would not be considered sinful for a person of lesser moral stature, but for Jacob it is sinful. This relatively minor transgression, a fault not perceived by Jacob himself, is unworthy of him and is harshly punished. The "slamming" of the door was motivated by a force embedded very deeply in the unconscious and was regarded by the sages as a valid reason for punishment.

KORAH'S REBELLION

The fourth book of the Old Testament (Numbers, Chapters 16 and 17) contains the story of Korah (Korach) who led a rebellion against Moses' and Aaron's leadership. The rebels claimed that they were altruistically motivated. They argued that all Israel is holy and sanctified and criticized Moses and Aaron for being haughty. Nahmanides (Ramban, a biblical commentator second only to Rashi) explains (16:5) that Korah was able to win a following by promising to restore the priestly duties to the firstborn, as was the case before Aaron and his sons were chosen for this role. Korah denied that God chose Aaron and implied that Moses lied in saying that Aaron was chosen by Him. Moses, however, was able to discern that Korah was motivated by jealousy; he coveted the priesthood. Korah was not a simple person. The sages speak very highly of his wisdom. They were puzzled by his behavior and asked, "Why did the wise Korah indulge in such silliness?" How could he doubt that Moses, who had led them out of Egypt, performed miracles, ascended Mt. Sinai, and was God's messenger to give and teach Torah, was not telling the truth? They resolved the dilemma by stating that the pious Korah was able to gaze into the future. He saw that the great prophet Samuel was one of his descendants. Incidentally, the fact that he was able to gaze into the future attests to his spiritual stature.[10] He, however, did not realize that this ability was not necessarily attrib-

---

10. Korah was not a prophet. Jewish thought postulates a level of spirituality called *ruach hakodesh,* literally "holy spirit" which enables the person attaining it to see or rather to know the future. This is a limited ability; even prophecy on a higher level is not to be understood as a force endowing the prophet to "see" the future. The prophet "sees" only what is shown to him/her. Korah gazed into the future, but erred in his interpretation of what he saw.

utable to him, to his merit. His sons did not follow him; they repented, and it is to their merit that a distinguished line of spiritual leaders were descended from them. They, the sons, composed a number of psalms bearing their name in the book of Psalms (*Tehillim*). Rabbi Levovitz[11] astutely comments that despite Korah's greatness, despite his ability to gaze into the future, he was not able or rather did not wish to examine his own psyche, to try and grasp his own underlying motivations, to examine the purity of his own motives. This led to his downfall. The sages viewed his rebellion as an example of controversy not purely motivated, in contrast to the halakhic disputes between the sages Hillel and Shamai. Controversy, criticism, is not in itself a blemish, a wrongdoing to be avoided. It is reprehensible when it is hypocritical, when it is selfishly motivated, when it is employed to dethrone ethical values and God's dictates. Furthermore, argues Rabbi Levovitz, Korah's rebuke of Moses was not intrinsically wrong. We find that Jethro also challenged and criticized Moses. The flaw lies in the motivation. At the root of Korah's criticism, jealousy reared its ugly head. Moses, following God's wishes, appointed Elitzaphon, the son of Uziel, to a higher position than Korah. Korah's pride was involved. Even this can, under certain circumstances, be viewed favorably. If one is motivated by a desire to serve the Almighty more intensely by holding a position requiring a closer relationship in service to Him, it is not a blemish. However, Korah was not motivated by purely spiritual reasons. Simple jealousy, which was not discerned or acknowledged— as a result of a failure to examine the depths of his personality, to discover the unconscious reasons for his actions—prompted his rebellion. Korah did not, perhaps, consciously set out to rebel, but he was led by his un-

---

11. *Daat Chochma Umussar*, vol. 1, p. 205.

conscious, unacknowledged jealousy. For a person of his moral stature, the failure to delve into the unconscious and seek out the hidden reasons for his actions is sinful and led to the acts which earned him eternal infamy.

NADAV AND AVIHU—AARON'S SONS

The story of Nadav and Avihu, Aaron's sons who were punished by death, is stated simply and starkly in Leviticus 10:1. The exact nature of their transgression is debated by the sages.[12] There is no question that it was a major sin, warranting the punishment meted out to them. In spite of this, they are acknowledged to be spiritual giants, greater in some respects than Moses and Aaron.[13] How can we understand this intriguing tale? How can we reconcile the severity of their punishment with the pronouncement that they were extraordinary people? As a first step, it is important to realize that the sages judged people's actions by the following principle: Evaluation and judgment of behavior are relative, not absolute. Although there is no distinction between people as to their obligation to heed the Torah's positive and negative commandments, there is no divine universal scale of rewards and punishment equally applicable to all. The actions of one individual may be ignored or even praised, but the same action may be condemned when performed by a different person from whom a higher level of conduct is expected.[14]

---

12. See 'Klai Yokar' for a brief listing and discussion of this debate. The exact nature of the sin is not relevant to the discussion. This commentary is found in many Hebrew printings of the Bible.

13. Rashi (10:3), who quotes the sages.

14. Chasman, Yehuda L. (1973). *Or Yohail*, vol. 2, pp. 49–51. Jerusalem: See also Rabbi Hayim (1985). *Bayurai Rabbainu Hayim M'Volozhin*, p. 65. Jerusalem: Rabbi Hayim explains why there are different standards of conduct and, consequently, of punishment for different individuals. Some people are endowed with greater spiritual faculties (*neshamot*–souls), thus more is expected of them. They are held to a higher standard of conduct and their transgressions are viewed more harshly. This principle is accepted by the Hasidic masters as well. The most famous disciple of the Baal Shem Tov (Besht), the founder of Hasidism, was Rabbi Ber, the *Magid* of Mezritch. He taught that the improper thoughts of holy people cause greater harm, in a spiritual sense (in higher spiritual worlds), than even the gravest

Culpability and responsibility relate not only to the action, but to the person who performed it. This approach was extended by the Mussar school to the text. They interpreted the Torah's language to reflect this principle.[15] The Torah depicts the relatively minor transgressions of highly respected spiritual leaders, people of high moral stature, in language normally used to describe the gravest transgressions.[16]

Nadav and Avihu were saintly people and were therefore expected to act in corresponding fashion. They were also human, subject to mundane pressures. Under the special scrutiny reserved for people of high moral stature, their reaction to that human layer of pressure was labeled a transgression and mandated punishment. The Torah cannot and does not wish to conceal or gloss over a transgression which, if perpetrated by others, would probably not be considered sinful. Torah is truth and truth is uncompromising. This high standard dictates that their action be considered sinful and be depicted in harsh terms reserved for gross sins. The Torah reveals and uncovers defects which may be unknown to the doer, lodged as they are in the unconscious, in the deepest layers of personality.

---

transgressions of simpler people. Rabbi Ber of Mezritch, *Torat Hamagid*, ed. Y. Klapholtz, p. 45. Bnai Brak.

15. Natan Z. Finkel, *Or Hatzafun*, vol. 1 (Jerusalem: Mosad Haskail Yeshivat Hebron, 1959). essay no. 33.

16. Eliyuhu E. Dessler, *Michtov M'Eliyuhu*, vol. 1 (London: Comm. for the Publication of the Writings of Rabbi Dessler, 1955), pp. 161–166. Rabbi Dessler's writings have since been republished many times. He points to the language used in Joshua chapter 7:11. The statement "Israel has sinned and abrogated my covenant" is phrased in the plural, although only one person, Ochon, sinned. The severity of sin is measured by the harm it causes and the moral stature of the perpetrator. Therefore, in that instance, it is as if all Israel had sinned. Another example is the sin of the golden calf. The Torah accuses the entire nation (Exodus 32:7), although only 3,000 people actually worshipped the idol, the number given of those who died (32:28).

ISRAEL'S FORTY YEARS OF WANDERING IN THE DESERT

The generation which was redeemed from Egyptian slavery and expired in the desert provides additional examples of how useful the concept of the unconscious is as a tool to aid our understanding. Maimonides (Rambam) and Nahmanides (Ramban) agree that the men and women of that generation were of exemplary character. They attained a level of prophecy greater than that of the prophet Ezekiel.[17] Nevertheless, the Torah records their constant bickering and sinning, which ultimately led to their being denied entry to the promised land. This enigma can be understood by employing the concept of the unconscious as the basis of a theoretical framework with which to approach the issue. They were extraordinary people who were privileged to be at Sinai and hear the Almighty proclaim the Ten Commandments. They witnessed miracles. These prerogatives can be granted only to the very worthy. However, their greatness prescribed for them a level of conduct far above that expected from ordinary people. Their greatness was their undoing. At their spiritual level, even a small blemish is magnified and considered grave. We can now apply the principle of the unconscious. Their errors were not the sort one witnesses in simple, ordinary folk, in spite of the fact that the Torah castigates them and portrays them in harsh terms more applicable to ordinary sinners and sins.[18] Having established that they

---

17. Ramban in his commentary (Numbers 19:8) quotes Maimonides and agrees with him on this point. They base their contention on a talmudic teaching. See also Ramban's commentary (Deuteronomy 8:2). He notes that this generation subsisted on heavenly bread 'manna,' a privilege not accorded to others including the patriarchs and matriarchs.

18. The 'Netziv,' the revered dean of the Yeshiva in Volozhin during the latter half of the 19th century, has this to say on this subject.

were not simple people, easily led astray, the concept of
the unconscious can resolve the enigma. There are
thoughts, wishes, desires unknown to the conscious which
originate in the deeper layers of personality, in the unconscious. These are not readily known or understood, but
are potent forces guiding an individual's behavior. It be-
hooves the individual to search deeply, to be able to comprehend the roots of his/her behavior. The greater the
person, the greater his/her responsibility to constantly
question him/herself, asking if the motivating forces stem
from pure sources or are tainted by personal, selfish, or
immoral considerations. The high moral stature of that
generation shouldered them with the awesome responsibility of continually subjecting themselves to repeated self-
examination. It was in this area that they apparently failed
in that they did not detect that their behavior was at times
motivated by improper considerations. The sages succinctly characterize God's relationship with the pious: "the
Almighty is extraordinarily meticulous in His accounting
with the very pious." [19]

Rabbi Naftali Zvi Berlin, *Haamek Dovar* (Jerusalem: El Hamekorot,
1959), Introduction. That generation was governed, meaning in respect
to God's relation to them, by different rules than those operating in
usual circumstances. He calls this *tiferet*. He defines this as a code
which calls for immediate punishment of transgressions.

19. Talmud, Yevomot 121b. The fourth chapter of the classical
ethical work, *Mesilat Yeshorim* (The Path of the Just) by Rabbi Moshe
Hayim Luzzatto, deals at length with this principle.

THE CONCEPT OF THE UNCONSCIOUS IN HASIDIC LITERATURE

Hasidic literature, except for a few exceptions, is not organized in systematic fashion. It does not deal with concepts in a manner similar to ethical or philosophical writings. It is usually presented to the reader as a compilation of comments on the Torah, each comment dealing with the text singled out, often mentioning and explaining other texts to emphasize an idea or to show its relation to other texts. Some Hasidic thinkers devoted their works to specific subjects, such as the holidays but there, as well, the form expressing their thinking is usually a text containing many interpretations. Rarely is there a text devoted to a specific subject, addressing itself to diverse aspects of the issue. This description also applies to the treatment of the unconscious. There is no systematic treatment of the concept. One looks in vain for a term to indicate the unconscious as, for example, the terms "inner" or "dormant forces" used in the Mussar movement. There are, however, clear indications that the concept was not foreign to Hasidic thought and was accepted and used by them as an interpretive tool. This was shown in the previous chapter and additional examples follow.

The Bible (Genesis, Chapter 18) relates the story of Abraham and the angels sent to inform him of the coming birth of his son Isaac. He was told that Sarah, who was barren and at an advanced age, would conceive and give birth to a son. Sarah overheard the conversation and laughed inwardly, for which she was reprimanded by God. At first, she denied that she had laughed, leading God to repeat His reprimand. Rabbi L. Eiger explains the incident by invoking a principle frequently used by Hasidic thinkers.[20] Sarah's initial denial and subsequent accep-

---

20. Rabbi Yehuda Leib Eiger (1889/1970). *Torat Emet,* vol. 1, p. 11. Bnai Brak: Yahadut.

tance of her laughter implies that, although she sinned, her acceptance rectified her faulty behavior (*tikun*) and she emerged absolved. This incident serves as a paradigm for later generations. It shows the way, in a deeper sense paves the way, for future men and women to more easily rectify their misdeeds. In developing this theme, he writes that Sarah's laughter was a conscious action on her part to belittle her importance, in that she was not worthy of such a miracle. The Almighty's censure teaches that, although on a conscious level her laughter was understandable, perhaps even praiseworthy, on a deeper level her laughter was also motivated, unknown to her consciously, by a measure of disbelief. This part of Rabbi Eiger's explanation is an example of the unconscious workings of the mind.

The second example is a terse comment by Rabbi Alter (Rim), the founder of the Hasidic dynasty of Gur, considered to be the movement with the greatest number of adherents (Hasidim) in Europe prior to the Holocaust. The story of the golden calf as told in Chapter 32 of Exodus is well known. However, it is difficult to comprehend. How is it possible that an entire nation which, just a short while ago, had witnessed miracles and stood at the foot of Mt. Sinai, could bring themselves to worship an idol? Much has been written by the classical Jewish Bible commentators to address this question. The consensus is that they did not believe that the calf was God, but rather that it represented Him. This, of course, casts a different light on the incident but, nevertheless, their fall bears explaining. It is not the present writer's intention or purpose to summarize the explanations offered, but rather, as noted above, to demonstrate that Hasidic thought recognizes the concept of the unconscious. The Rim addressed one aspect of the issue.[21] The sages taught that the Jews, be-

---

21. Rabbi Yitzhol M. Alter (1965). *Chidushai Horim Al Hatorah,* p. 106. Jerusalem: Nahalal Publishing Co.

fore entering into the covenant with God at Sinai, expressed their wish to follow God and walk in His ways, even prior to their knowledge of what this commitment entailed.[22] This attachment and devotion to Him compounds the dilemma. The Rim states that, despite the obviously high spiritual level they achieved upon entering into the covenant without knowing what was asked of them, something was lacking. They were not, says the Rim, on such a high spiritual level. Their willingness was not completely authentic. Reaching out to a level which in actuality is not the true measure of one's devotion is an act lacking in spiritual honesty. They were not conscious of this. However, it was deeply embedded in their psyche. This slight blemish planted the roots of future spiritual failure. This analysis demonstrates the perception of human character as a complex entity having its roots deeply embedded in the unconscious.

---

22. The sages in the Talmud (Shabbat 88b) teach that the willingness of the entire nation to enter into the covenant without knowing what it obligated them to do is the high point of that generation's spiritual level. The angels crowned each Jew with two crowns. Another sage teaches that a voice from heaven (*bat kol*) was heard asking, who divulged this secret (i.e., the willingness to accept God's yoke without at first ascertaining what it required) to my children.

5

The Challenge of Flawed Character Traits

A popular and highly valued commentary on the Mishna, *Tiferet Yisroel* was written by Rabbi Lifshitz in the late nineteenth century[1]. One of his comments evoked a heated controversy over a hundred years ago. This chapter deals with one aspect of that controversy. Is having the opinion that Moses was born with flawed character traits disrespectful and detractful of his stature?

---

1. The Mishna is the basis of the "oral law." It consists of six books and contains the teachings of the *tanaim,* the sages whose interpretations of Torah are incorporated in the Mishna. Originally oral law was forbidden to be written and was committed to memory. Rabbi Judah the Prince (Rav Yehuda Hanasi) realized that it was in danger of being forgotten. He, therefore, edited it and permitted it to be written. The Mishna is the basis of the Talmud, which is the teachings of the *Amoroim* who commented on and interpreted the Mishna. The term Mishna refers both to the six books and to individual *mishnayot,* consisting at times of only a few lines. The written Mishna dates from approximately the second century, the Talmud from approximately the fifth century. The Talmud contains many tractates.

The last Mishna in tractate Kidushin states that even the best physician is destined to be punished in the coming world. Rabbi Lifshitz interprets this as referring only to arrogant physicians who do not consult with their colleagues and/or do not refer to their texts, relying only on their knowledge. If, however, a physician is humble, is aware of his/her imperfections, and is willing to learn from others, the physician will be handsomely rewarded in the next world. In support of his interpretation, he relates the following story.

Israel's release from Egyptian bondage under the leadership of Moses caused a tremendous stir. The nations of the world were highly impressed. They felt that Moses had accomplished the impossible and were very curious, wanting to know what sort of person he is. A noted monarch sent an artist to paint his portrait. He believed that an analysis of his features would reveal Moses' character. The portrait was painted and presented to the king and his wise men. Their conclusions based on the portrait were that Moses is an unsavory, arrogant person. They could not detect even one pleasant praiseworthy trait. The king expressed his displeasure which prompted the artist to claim that the wise men erred, and the wise men to question the painter's artistic ability. The king went to meet Moses and was astonished when he saw that the painting was an accurate portrait of Moses. He spoke to Moses, observed his interaction with people and concluded that Moses was a saintly person. The king then shared his feelings of disappointment and chagrin as to the wisdom of his advisors with Moses. Moses calmed the king and informed him that his advisors are competent and did not err. Moses explained that the portrait is an accurate description of the traits with which he was endowed, but that with superhuman effort he succeeded in overcoming those traits.

The controversy that erupted involved two points:[2] (a) Is the story historically correct? Rabbis Rapaport and Rabinowitz-Teomim claimed that the story's roots are pagan and it is not a correct representation of Jewish history or Jewish spirit; and (b) a more important basic question: Is it disrespectful to claim that Moses was born with evil attributes? On this point as well, Rabbis Rapaport and Rabinowitz-Teomim (Aderet) felt very strongly that Moses was, from birth, saintly and of sterling character, and criticized Rabbi Lifshitz for what they considered disrespect towards Moses. However, the premise that Moses was much less than perfect at birth seems to have been accepted in Hasidic circles and found a supporter among the Russian Lithuanian rabbinate in the person of Rabbi Yosef Zechaya Stern, one of the leading Talmudic authorities of his time. The issues, aside from their intrinsic interest, are important because of their relevance to those discussed in Chapter 2. It will be recalled that the discussion centered on the question of how to construe man's–woman's basic nature.

---

2. This chapter is based upon an article by Shneur Z. Leiman, (Summer 1989). "The Portrait of Moses," *Tradition* 29(4): 91–98. It also includes my comments on his article published in the Fall 1991 issue of the same journal, *Tradition* 26(1), and his rebuttal. This chapter is an enlarged and revised version of my critique.

RELEVANT PSYCHOLOGICAL THEORIES

The leading psychological theories explaining human nature were reviewed in Chapter 2. The following is a brief and concise summary. Freud and Konrad Lorenz believe that aggression is a built-in characteristic of human nature. The renowned exponents of the humanist school, Maslow and Rogers, see man–woman as basically good or, at the least, neutral. Rollo May, representing the existentialist branch of the humanists, feels that Rogers errs in not recognizing the depth and pervasiveness of evil found in people. These approaches reflect positions articulated by philosophers and serious thinkers throughout the ages. The question whether true altruism exists was also discussed as being relevant to the discussion, and the empirical findings of social psychologists on this issue as well as that of aggression were noted.

ARGUMENTS CRITICAL AND SUPPORTIVE OF THE TIFERET'S POSITION

The eminent Rabbi Rabinowitz-Teomim, known as the Aderet, in his letter to Rabbi Rapaport, who instigated the controversy, had this to say:[3]

> I have often rebuked those who quoted the Tiferet and have publicly proclaimed that the Tiferet erred. He relied on pagan sources thereby belittling the sanctity of the most righteous person of all.

He supports Rabbi Rapaport's arguments based on the sages' teachings purporting to show that Moses was devoid of blemish at birth.[4] As further proof, he quotes the Talmud (Megillah 11:a), which states that "Aaron and Moses were righteous from beginning to end." One may argue, and it is probable that this is what Rabbis Lifshitz and Stern felt, that the arguments presented do not prove that Moses was born without fault. They do unequivocally show that he was very special when born, possessing reservoirs of spiritual strength and holiness. This, however, does not necessarily mean that he was faultless. This line of reasoning is found in one of the early Hasidic writers,

---

3. Rabbi Eliyuhu D. Rabinowitz-Teomim in his letter to Rabbi Rapaport printed in the latter's pamphlet, *Zechus Horabim* (Jerusalem: 1894).

4. Ibid. In his pamphlet, Rabbi Rapaport presents (as one of many arguments) the verse (Exodus 2:2) "She saw that he was good" which the sages understand as meaning that the house was suffused with light when Moses was born, quoted by Rashi in his comment on that verse. Rabbi Rapaport's argument is that the term 'good' denotes goodness in all its aspects. The pamphlet also contains arguments by Rabbi Y. L. Diskin, considered a giant in his era, proving that the supposed event could not have happened.

Rabbi Moshe Hayim Ephrayim, a grandson of the founder
of Hasidism, the Baal Shem Tov (Besht).[5]

> The Israelites saw that his face (Moses) emitted a shin-
> ing light. I have been privileged by the Almighty to com-
> prehend the deep secrets of this verse based upon my
> grandfather's (the Besht, Baal Shem Tov) teachings. He
> explained a difficult talmudic saying that the Jews were
> asked (on a different occasion) whether Moses was a
> vagabond or thief. Another talmudic saying which
> bears explaining is that some Jews harbored a suspi-
> cion that Moses committed grave sins. My grandfather
> of blessed memory explained that our teacher Moses
> was born with a natural inclination towards wicked-
> ness, brimming with vices. However, he overcame them
> and labored to instill in himself saintly desirable
> traits. . . . This (the following thoughts are those of the
> grandson) explains why some viewed Moses as a sin-
> ner, they saw only the inborn traits. This changed
> when Moses descended from Mt. Sinai, his face bathed
> in light. They then understood that he had managed
> to transmute vices into virtues. He was born possess-
> ing desirable characteristics which, however, at that
> time were 'hidden.'[6]

---

5. Rabbi Moshe Hayim Ephrayim, *Degel Machne Ephrayim*
(Jerusalem: Publishing house and date not given), pp. 81–82. The *Degel*
is a Hasidic classic and has been reprinted many times. The quote is
from his comments on the last verse of Chapter 34 in the Book of
Exodus.

6. Professor Leiman wrote in his article (note no. 2), "this early
view of Moses appears to have no parallel in classical Talmudic or
Midrashic literature, nor do kabbalistic sources seem to support such
a view regarding Moses." In my comments I pointed out that the Degel
portrays Moses as endowed from birth with both the most saintly virtues and highly detrimental traits. In his rebuttal Professor Leiman
claims that this perception of Moses is that of the grandson, not necessarily that of the grandfather, the Besht. This does not seem to be
a reasonable thesis. Nowhere in hasidic literature do we find an opinion which may be construed, even very slightly, as deviating from the

It is quite clear that his position is that Moses was endowed with opposing sets of characteristics; at birth only the baser traits were apparent. This accounts for the fact that at times Moses was misunderstood and suspected of immoral behavior. This, however, leaves us with the task of explaining the fact that when Moses was born, the house became ablaze with light.[7] This seems to contradict the premise that only the baser traits were seen or evident at birth.[8] Perhaps, in spite of his being endowed with grave character faults, his potential holiness was so pervasive and powerful that it shone forth.

One of the foremost disciples of the Besht, Rabbi Jacob Joseph, is the author of the first published book of Hasidic Bible interpretations. He quotes his teacher's explanation to a different verse than that expounded upon by the Degel, but based upon the same premise—that Moses was endowed with both good and base traits.[9] He informs us that the Besht taught that Moses himself questioned the purity of his personality, his righteousness. He suspected that he personified evil forces. This situation, this relentless self-questioning, was, rather paradoxically, a function of his great spiritual stature. He encompassed within his person the entire cosmos, which includes both good and evil. How, then, Moses reasoned, could he ex-

---

Besht's views, certainly so when a grandson writes that his thoughts are based upon his grandfather's premises. Furthermore, additional sources confirming that the hasidic masters felt that Moses was endowed with both good and bad traits, will be presented.

7. See note no. 4.

8. This problem was addressed by a hasidic thinker in his book first published in the first half of the 19th century—Rabbi Moshe Sofer, *Or Penai Moshe* (Israel: Publisher and date not noted), pp. 76–77, Book of Numbers. He writes that the light was a prophetic one. His mother was shown or told that Moses would overcome his earthiness and shine in a remarkable way.

9. Quoted in *Baal Shem Tov Al Hatorah*, ed. Shimon M. Mandel, vol. 2 (Jerusalem: 1971), p. 6.

emplify sanctity and the glorification of God's name? This issue is resolved by invoking a principle known metaphorically as 'the evil is the chair of the good,' meaning that ultimate goodness, the pinnacle of holiness, must undergo rites of passage through evil.[10]

Rabbi Shlomo Lutzker writes that Moses, by virtue of his holiness, was able to overcome his inclination toward wickedness and his vices.[11] He adds a novel explanation as to why Moses was saddled with this burden. Moses was conceived and born in holiness. However, the fact that his parents formed a union which, in the future, when the Torah would be given to Israel, was prohibited [Yocheved was Amram's aunt], this tainted him. At an even deeper level, he postulates that this was necessary. The *Tzadik*, the holy person, can be of assistance to others, can help them in their spiritual struggles, only if he shares with them a common denominator.[12] The above references, as

---

10. Ibid. See also footnote no. 6 on page 7 of the above. Other great hasidic thinkers are quoted who affirm the principle that pure goodness has to experience evil and overpower it, and then apply this to Moses. One of the giants of hasidism, Rabbi Elimelech of Lizansk, taught that Moses wished to completely purify himself and was told by God that this is not possible. Only when the era of the "end of days" will arrive can that goal be achieved. He interprets the enigma of the burning bush which was not consumed, and had attracted and fascinated Moses (Exodus 3:2), as demonstrating this principle. Moses wished to attain ultimate purity and spirituality; this is the significance of the fire. He attained this ardent desire to serve God, this inner fire. Nevertheless, the thorns exemplifying the impure traits were not completely consumed by the fire, teaching him, as noted above, that complete purity is not attainable in this world.

11. Rabbi Shlomo Lutzker, *Divrat Shlomo* (Zalkuva: 1848), Parshat Vayikra Leviticus, p. 1.

12. The concept of the Tzadik is a central one in hasidic thought. It is linked to the principle that people are bound to and responsible for one another. The Tzadik and his role is the subject of extensive discussions in hasidic literature. For example, see: Rabbi Elimelech of Lizansk, *Noam Elimelech* (Jerusalem: Publisher and date not noted) Exodus Shemot, and Rabbi Menachem Mendel of Vitebsk, *Pri Haretz*

well as others cited in the footnotes, establish that Hasidic thinkers perceived Moses as being in possession of great potential for both good and evil at birth.[13] Rabbi Elimelech seems to imply that even in maturity, Moses was tainted.[14] True, he reached the pinnacle, but being human it was not possible to cleanse himself completely.[15]

(Jerusalem: 1974), p. 101. Rabbi Menachem ties the concept of the Tzadik to the concept of "impurity leading to purity."

13. See also *Or Hachayim* commentary on Torah. In one passage (Deuteronomy 33:4) he writes that Moses attained exemplary traits because of his "Yirat Shomayim," the fear of God. In a different passage (Exodus 3:4) he states explicitly that Moses was destined for prophecy prior to birth. This indicates that he, as well, is of the opinion that Moses had both tendencies, both characteristics. His good traits came about because and due to his fear of God, implying that it was not a natural sequence of events, that he had to toil mightily to incorporate good traits in his personality. On the other hand, he was chosen to be a prophet, the most important prophet, even before birth.

14. Rabbi Elimelech of Lizansk, note no. 10.

15. Being human means that even the most spiritual are not completely free of materialistic tendencies and, therefore, are bound to traits associated with earthiness. In chapter 3 (The Unconscious) a similar concept of Rabbi Salanter was discussed.

THEOLOGICAL AND PSYCHOLOGICAL
IMPLICATIONS

The principle that good and evil tendencies (inclinations) must be balanced was discussed in Chapter 2. A person must be in a position to freely choose one over the other. Any other arrangement of the balance of power precludes a just decision insofar as divine reward and punishment of behavior is concerned. This is a cardinal principle of Judaism. Having established and accepted this principle, we are presented with a dilemma. Why were eminent rabbis (Rabinowitz-Teomim and Rapaport) distressed at the implication that Moses was born less than perfect? Certainly even Moses had to resist the evil inclination so as to be able to reach the highest spiritual level attainable and be rewarded for this achievement. One can conjecture that they would argue that holding the opinion that Moses was born with an innate tendency towards wickedness is not quite the same as believing that all mature people are exposed to equally powerful virtuous and evil inclinations. A distinction must be made between an evil inclination which is part of the human condition and innate wicked characteristics or traits. The other equally eminent rabbis and Hasidic leaders seem to be saying that, since even Moses had to contend with an evil inclination it is not disrespectful to maintain that his personality, his psychological makeup, was, from birth, laced with vices.[16] On the contrary, this condition is what renders Moses uniquely fitted to become the redeemer, the

---

16. The basic idea that evil is a springboard to virtue is also found in the Gra's commentaries. He writes that rewards in the coming world are based upon "turning the bitter into sweet." This is phrased differently than the concept espoused by the hasidic masters and may be expressing a different emphasis, but the basic idea seems similar: Rabbi Eliyuhu of Vilna, *Orot Hagra* (Bnai Brak: Kollel Tel Ganim, 1986), p. 74.

intermediary between God and Israel. His everlasting greatness resides in his struggle to attain a supreme level of holiness. That struggle was singular in that it did not form a barrier separating him from others. By overcoming the obstacles, he was infused with unparalleled spirituality, forging a common bond with ordinary people that allowed him to reach out and be of help to them.

In his letter to R. Rapaport mentioned above, the Aderet directs his attention to the Rambam's (Maimonides) famous principle found in the sixth chapter of his introduction to the "Sayings of the Fathers," *Pirkai Avot*. The Rambam discusses the debate between philosophers as to who is on a higher spiritual plane, a person who overcomes his evil inclination or the individual who has no desire to sin. He concludes that this question can be resolved by considering the nature of the transgression. He distinguishes between a sin considered reprehensible by people because it violates common decency and accepted moral behavior, for example, murder, thievery, or abuse of one's parents; and actions which are sinful because they are prohibited by the Torah. Both categories are prohibited and one must overcome the desire to sin. However, a wish to act contrary to the Torah's prohibition of sins in the latter category is not indicative of a tarnished soul, whereas the desire to murder, steal, etc. is, in itself, unworthy. The Aderet argues that, in placing the 'Hasid' (one who has no desire to sin) above the *Moshail Berucho* (one who overcomes the desire), insofar as sins violating the accepted codes of morality and decency are concerned, the Rambam proves that Moses was not tainted with flawed character traits (which, according to the story recounted by the Tiferet, included all vices). We do not find a rebuttal in the writings of the other camp; it seems that they did not address themselves to this problem. We, therefore, must assume that the Aderet's comments and the question he raised did not seem problematic to them. They certainly knew the Rambam's principle, but did not feel that it contradicted their position. It is reasonable to assume they felt that the philosophical debate reported by the Rambam and his solution were not relevant to the question. The Rambam's analysis pertains to mature individuals; the question they dealt with was the character makeup of Moses at birth. As was pointed out, their position is that, in spite of the fact that he was born with an innate propensity to wickedness, he overcame this tendency, transforming himself into a virtual reservoir of goodness and virtue. This, they would argue, is what made him so great.[17]

---

17. The correspondence between Rabbis Rapaport and Aderet included a discussion as to whether a "baal-teshuva," a pentinent, is considered worthier than a "tzadik," one who hasn't sinned. Rabbi Rabinowitz-Teomim contends that the issue is not relevant since Moshe Rabainu hadn't sinned. However, other comments by the Aderet are not quite clear. For example, he singles out the concept of the sages that Moses and Aaron were righteous throughout their entire lives. It seems as if he understood R. Lifshitz as saying that Moses sinned (i.e., aside from the inborn base character traits) during his youth. However, nowhere does Rabbi Lifshitz advance such a claim. Perhaps the Aderet is of the opinion that arguing that Moses was born with grave character defects is tantamount to saying that he sinned. This seems far-fetched.

COMPARING THE JEWISH AND PSYCHOLOGICAL VIEWS

The controversy between the two camps of Jewish think-ers seems similar to the two conflicting psychological positions as to the nature of man–woman. The thinkers who felt that Moses was tainted at birth with grave char-acter defects are theoretically equivalent to the psycholo-gists who view humans as essentially evil. The others who vehemently opposed the notion that Moses was born with innate evil tendencies, could be equated with those psy-chologists who see people as being basically good. It was, however, pointed out that the controversy among Jewish scholars is confined to Moses' psychological makeup at birth and is specific to Moses and the unique position he occupies in history. This seems to rule out the above com-parison, since we are dealing with different issues. Nev-ertheless, it can reasonably be maintained that the Hasidic thinkers and their rabbinic counterparts would agree that people have a large measure of innate evil. Their percep-tion of evil as a path toward virtue would leave them less disturbed at this possibility than the other camp.

This line of reasoning directs us to consider another point. Hjelle and Ziegler count changeability–unchangeability as one of the basic issues dividing psy-chologists. They write:[18]

> The basic issue involved in this assumption is the de-gree to which the individual is seen as capable of fun-damental change throughout life. That is, can an individual's basic personality makeup really change to a large degree over time? Going a step farther, is ba-sic change a necessary component in the evolution or

---

18. Larry A. Hjelle and Daniel J. Ziegler, *Personality Theories*, 2nd Ed. (New York: McGraw-Hill, 1981), pp. 17–18.

development of personality? Or are the surface changes in behavior that occur superficial while the basic underlying personality structure remains unalterable and intact. . . . Even theorists within the same broad tradition can be found to be at odds with one another on this issue. To wit, both Sigmund Freud and Erik Erikson clearly represent the psychoanalytic tradition within personality theory, yet they profoundly disagree on this basic assumption. Erikson assumes a much greater degree of changeability in personality than does Freud.

The issue of changeability–nonchangeability can serve to illuminate the controversy between those who felt that Moses was born with character defects and those who oppose this view. It was noted above that the Aderet felt that the Rambam's pronouncement that, insofar as actions contrary to morality are concerned, the Hasid (who has no desire to sin) is on a higher spiritual level than the person who overcomes the wish to sin supports the position that Moses was born pure. It was argued that the other thinkers would probably maintain that the Rambam is referring to mature people, whereas their position is that although Moses was born flawed, he did not succumb to sin and transformed the flaws into virtues. This reasoning seems so self-evident, that it is difficult to understand what prompted the Aderet to think the Rambam supported his position. Perhaps this is what he meant. If Moses was born flawed, then it seems that others are certainly born with a tendency to do evil. At this point, the issue of changeability is relevant and brought to bear on the issue. If a person is born with a large dose of evil and it is maintained that change is not easily effected, then a pessimistic position is assumed. This is not acceptable to the Aderet. Better to see Moses as pure and by extension others, although not in the same category as Moses. The other thinkers can hold one of two positions: (a) True,

Moses was born tainted; but this does not necessarily mean that others are also born impure. On the contrary, as was explained above, only Moses was born flawed, so that he might overcome those flaws and thereby reach the highest spiritual level; or (b) they can maintain that all people are born with evil as part of their personality composition; and that all people are malleable and open to change. They can, for example, adopt the position, later propounded by Erikson, that a person's developmental cycles allow him/her many opportunities to change.

The importance attached to the issue of man's nature and his/her genetic endowment is shared by both Judaism and psychology. There is, however, a basic difference between them as to the emphases each brings to the analysis of the problem. Psychology confines itself to attempting to understand people; this is the range of its interest. Judaism, indeed all religions and most philosophical systems, are interested in and attach great significance to the moral–ethical consequences of the issue. Religion sees the inculcation of moral–ethical values as its calling. It seeks to find ways to bring the person closer to spiritual values.[19] This is not so for psychology. Judaic literature, Talmud, and Midrash, contain many discussions related to the concept of the inclinations analyzing their

---

19. This has a twofold purpose: (a) to purify the individual; (b) to enable God's majesty to be revealed. Two thinkers explain the second process in similar fashion. One, Rabbi Dessler, was a leading representative, in the first half of this century, of the mussar school— Rabbi Eliyuhu E. Dessler, "*Michtov M'Eliyuhu,*" vol. 3 (Bnai Brak: Chever Talmiduv, 1965), p. 148. The other is one of the first hasidic masters, Rabbi Menachem Mendel of Vitebsk (note no. 12, pp. 97–98). They describe two ways in which God's name can be sanctified: (a) by turning flaws into virtues—the greater the flaw, the greater the sanctification of His name if and when the person succeeds in overcoming and conquering the evil. He turns darkness into light revealing God's majesty; (b) A virtuous person, humble and of flawless character, is the recipient of god's grace and thereby sanctifies His name.

influence. It also deals with the concept of character traits. There is a clear distinction between the two concepts, inclinations and traits. Psychology, on the other hand, whose interest is directed toward understanding behavior, has no need to distinguish between the two; indeed it does not recognize the concept of evil and good inclinations. Human behavior is perceived as directed and motivated by whatever systems a particular theory sees fit to adopt. Inclinations are not part of those systems; they imply theological connotations which are of no interest to psychology. Judaism, indeed most religions, strive to instill spirituality and obedience to the Divine will. Terms such as inclinations, good, evil, divine help, and grace are, in this context, meaningful terms. This is not so for psychology which does not consider this area its legitimate concern. For psychology, traits and inclinations are equivalent terms.

6

Psychotherapy

PSYCHOTHERAPY: ITS RELATION TO BIBLICAL AND RABBINIC JUDAISM

The interrelatedness of religion and psychotherapy has been extensively analyzed and research has been carried out on the specific ties between Judaism and psychotherapy. This chapter is a further exploration of some of the threads tying Judaism to the therapeutic process primarily as exemplified by depth psychology. The following issues form the basis of this study: What are the biblical and rabbinic concepts which bear an affinity to psychotherapy? How can therapeutic goals and methods be accommodated in the framework of *halakha* (Jewish law) and Jewish philosophy? Are there major therapeutic premises that are congenial to Judaic thought?

It is noteworthy that there are striking differences between writers who analyze the relation between psychotherapy and religion in general, and writers who study the specifically Jewish aspects of the topic. We do not, for example, find the former debating as to how to construe therapy. It is an accepted assumption that psychotherapy is perceived as a healing process. Indeed, Freud felt it necessary to declare that a psychoanalyst need not necessarily be a physician. Knight draws interesting parallels between the therapist and priest as healers.[1] He believes, drawing upon the teachings culled from the tales associated with the mythological image of Acklepios, that the patient has a healer within and the healer a patient within. It can be argued that the Rogerian emphases are at variance with a healer model, but that is beyond the scope of this paper. However, scholars who study the specifically Jewish aspects of therapy have advanced a number of differing theories as how to view psychotherapy. What accounts for this phenomenon and for the wide divergence of opinion on this issue? It seems to be a result of the fact that Judaism is not merely a faith to be embraced or a set of assumptions to believe in, but a way of life, mandated by rules—halakha—to be followed. This fosters an intellectual climate attuned to constantly probing and questioning whether contemplated moves and psychotherapeutic techniques and goals are halakhically compatible. These preoccupations prompted theorists to search for a framework, a model most suited to accommodate their concerns.

Kahn writes: "Within the framework of Jewish law (halakha) the concern and reaction to unacceptable behavior of others can be viewed from a number of perspectives. Broadly speaking, concern for the behavior of others falls under the general demand for mutual responsibility of *arevut* (which is the Hebrew word for responsibility, signifying the bond between individuals from which follows the obligation to be concerned and care for the other.

---

1. Knight, James A. (1986). "The Religio-Psychological Dimension of Wounded Healers," *Psychology of Religion*, ed. Lillian H. Robinson, pp. 33–49. Washington, D.C.: American Psychiatric Press.

A.R.). More specifically, however, the issue is crystallized in the obligation to reprove others for their wrongdoing–*hokeakh tohiakh.*"[2] The relevant biblical verse is:

> Thou shalt not hate thy brother in thy heart; thou shalt surely rebuke thy neighbor, and not bear sin because of him (Leviticus 19;17, Soncino Press. In this chapter all translations are Soncino).

Kahn quotes Mermelstein, who argued that reproof should not be perceived as merely a punitive judgmental process. However, Berger also quoted by Kahn took issue with Mermelstein. Kahn supports Mermelstein, citing sources indicating that reproof, when offered according to halakhic rules, is a caring procedure. This approach, as he notes, leads to thorny issues, which he discusses. Kahn's and other thinkers' resolutions of these issues are not relevant to the thesis of this discussion. His willingness to confront the implications, laudable as that may be, seems to this author to miss the point, which is; why is there a need to construct a model of therapy different from the accepted clinical-healing model?, a question not addressed in his paper.

Spero discusses "the validity of the notion that psychotherapeutic insights are similar to the Jewish concept of *viduy,* generally considered as confession. . . . On the other hand, confession is a conscious act or ritual designed expressly for repentance. It, therefore, involves the presumption of moral judgments on the act done. . . . In psychotherapy, one does not confess in the strict sense of the word. The goal of therapy is not to bring moral or religious judgment to bear on the confessed material. The

---

2. Kahn, Paul (1983). "Psychotherapy and the Commandment to Reprove." *Proceedings of the Association of Orthodox Jewish Scientists,* ed. Charles S. Naiman, pp. 37–49. New York: Sepher-Hermon Press Inc.

goal of therapy is purely relief from tension."[3] In a later publication, he presents other concepts as models to describe the role of the therapist and the process of therapy.[4] The concepts of repentance, rebuke, and confession are held to mirror or to have an affinity to some aspects of therapy. He does not, however, consider them as capturing the essence of therapy. His analysis stresses the need to objectify or schematize therapy in order to deal with particular techniques halakhically.

Of particular interest is his treatment of therapy as a 'healing process. He feels this analogy raises a number of issues. They range from basic theoretical problems such as: Does adopting a healing medical approach imply acceptance of psychological disorder as disease?, to other specific halakhic questions. He suggests other models which can serve as adjuncts to the helper model, specifically Linzer's model of *chesed*—loving-kindness—as a supplement to the healer model.[5]

It is surprising that a model of the therapist as educator and therapy as reeducation has not been proposed. This is congruent with Jewish thinking in which education and scholarship occupy the most prestigious roles. Moreover, this model is not foreign to others. As early as 1916, Oskar Pfister described psychoanalysis as a form of education and suggested that Freud was a great pedagogue.[6] Rogers viewed psychotherapy and education as

---

3. Spero, Moshe H. (1976). "On the Relationship Between Psychotherapy and Judaism." *Journal of Psychology and Judaism*, Fall 1:15–33.

4. ——— (1986). *Handbook of Psychotherapy and Jewish Ethics*, pp 1–28. Jerusalem: Feldheim.

5. Linzer, Norman (1979). "A Jewish Philosophy of Social Work Practice," *Journal of Jewish Communal Service* 55:309–317.

6. Ekstein, Rudolf and Motto, Rocco L. (1969). "Psychoanalysis and Education—An Historical Account." *From Learning for Love to Love of Learning*, ed. Rudolf Ekstein and Rocco L. Motto, p. 4. New York: Brunner/Mazel.

closely affiliated, hence his intense interest in education.[7]

The literature indicates the need to grapple with the task of finding a role model for psychotherapy in tune with Jewish tradition. This is so because of problems that may surface as a result of a true or perceived contradiction between some therapeutic goals and techniques and halakha. However, insofar as the fundamental issue is concerned, which is how to best construe or accommodate therapy with Judaic biblical and rabbinic sources, the controversy and difficulties encountered are artificial and uncalled for. There is no need to deviate from the accepted view that therapy is a healing, helping process (i.e., a medical model). This statement is not meant to negate or minimize the obligation and importance of contending and grappling with any inconsistency, real or perceived, between the practice of psychotherapy and halakha. This, however, is a distinct issue and should not becloud the basic task of viewing therapy in a context congruent with Judaism.

---

7. Rabinowitz, Aaron (1992). "Psychotherapy and Education." *Porat Yosef,* ed. Bezalel Safran and Eliyahu Safran, pp. 79–92. Hoboken, N.J.: Ktav.

BIBLICAL SOURCES FOR A HEALING, HELPING MODEL

The Torah refers specifically to God's healing and preventing sickness (Exodus 15:26; 23:25). There are also references to His blessing people with good health and fruitfulness (Leviticus 26:9; Deuteronomy 28:11). There is, however, only one mention of the physician practicing medicine. The verses refer to a quarrel in which a person is injured and is attended to by a physician:

> and shall cause him to be 'thoroughly healed' (Exodus 19:21).

The Babylonian Talmud (*Baba Kama* 85:A) explains this to mean that, in the case of an inflicted injury, the aggressor pays the doctor's fees. Nowhere, however, is it mentioned that healing the sick is an obligatory deed. True, the Torah is replete with stories of kind deeds and helping actions, but a specific commandment to heal the sick is nowhere invoked. This omission is noteworthy and bears explaining. The rabbis explain that the performance of good deeds is subsumed under the injunction to walk in God's ways:

> For if ye shall diligently keep all these commandments which I command you, to do it, to love the Lord your God, to walk in all His ways, and to cleave unto Him (Deuteronomy 11:22).
>
> After the Lord God shall ye walk, and Him shall ye fear, and His commandments shall ye keep, and unto His voice shall ye hearken, and Him shall ye serve, and unto Him shall ye cleave (Deuteronomy 13:5).

Walking in his ways is explained in the Talmud (Sotah 14:A) to mean adopting His traits: He clothes the naked;

therefore we should clothe them; in like fashion as He visits the sick, comforts the bereaved, and buries the dead, so we have to perform these deeds. The sages' clarification is quoted by Rashi, the greatest medieval Jewish commentator on the Torah, adding (Deuteronomy 13:5) that the injunction to perform acts of *chesed* (loving-kindness) is ordained by the phrase "and unto Him shall ye cleave." This comment places these acts on the highest spiritual level to which a human can aspire—to cleave unto the Almighty.

The distinction between two types of religious experiences—numinous encounters and mystical union—is relevant to this discussion.[8] It can be argued that the Judaic perception of the religious experience is closer to that described as a numinous encounter than to mystical union, a point which will be discussed in the last chapter. There are, however, trends in Jewish thought that view specific kinds of encounters between man and God in terms, language, and description akin to the phenomenon labeled mystical union. The Ramban (Nahmanides, medieval Talmudist and Bible commentator second only to Rashi) describes the personality and behavior of the saintly individual who attains the level of spirituality characterized above as cleaving unto God. He writes in his biblical commentary (Leviticus 18:4): ". . . and those who forsake all worldly preoccupations as if they don't have a material self, and all their thoughts are directed toward Godly concerns like the prophet Elijah, and cleave unto Him, will live forever in their bodily and spiritual forms as scripture relates concerning Elijah and as Jewish tradition dictates."

The passage in the Talmud quoted above, listing the acts of chesed, does not include healing the sick. This,

---

8. See: Barbour, Ian (1990). *Religion in An Age of Science*, p. 47. San Francisco: Harper & Row.

as previously noted, calls for an explanation. Nahmanides, in his commentary (Leviticus 26:11), explains God's promise to Israel that He will reside amongst them to mean that they will be healthy and will not require a physician's services. He quotes the following verse to prove his point:

> I will put none of the diseases upon thee, which I have put upon the Egyptians; for I am the Lord that healeth thee (Exodus 15:26).

He further states that, in the era of prophecy, a righteous person who fell sick would not seek a physician's services, but would turn to the prophet to ascertain the spiritual cause of his/her illness. Assa, king of Judah, is reprimanded because he availed himself of medical assistance when he became ill (Chronicles 2 16:1). According to Nahmanides, the verse in Exodus (19:21) quoted above permits the physician to minister to the patient's needs and entitles him to reimbursement. The physician should not refrain from doing so on the pretext that illness is God's punishment and therefore only He is permitted to heal. However, a righteous person during the prophetic era was obligated to turn to the prophet, not to the physician. To avert misunderstanding, it needs to be stressed that upon prophecy's decline, after the destruction of the First Temple, it became common practice to seek medical aid. Nahmanides himself, as well as Maimonides, was a practicing physician. Nahmanides' comment can explain why healing the sick is not enumerated as one of the acts of loving-kindness, since during the era of prophecy, a righteous person would not have turned to a physician. There is, however, no question that the physician to whom the sick turn to is walking in God's ways. The Almighty is the ultimate healer: ". . . for I am the Lord that healeth thee" (Exodus 15:26).

An additional point has to be clarified. Nahmanides' point that the Torah reassures the physician that practicing medicine is not negating God's intent seems relevant only in the case of physical ailments. In instances of emotional disturbance, however, the very nature of the illness precludes the knowledge and understanding necessary, on the part of the patient, to comprehend the severity of the illness and to be willing to turn to the prophet for guidance. In such situations it seems mandatory, even in the prophetic era, to seek assistance based on medical psychological knowledge and expertise.

Another biblical source is relevant to our discussion:

> Neither shalt thou stand idly by the blood of thy neighbor: I am the Lord (Leviticus 19:16).

This verse is interpreted to mean (Talmud, Sanhedrin 73:A) that one is obligated to come to the aid of an endangered person. Tendler writes: "This obligation even includes the assumption by the rescuer of financial expenditures. . . . It is therefore a biblical obligation for a family to accept the discomfort of meeting with the psychiatrist for counseling sessions to help a family member. Failure to do so is a violation of a series of positive and negative biblical and rabbinical precepts."[9] In sum, aiding a sick person is both a positive injunction subsumed under the principle of walking in God's ways and, if aid is not tendered, a violation of a negative commandment. Having established that a healing model of psychotherapy conforms to the biblical and rabbinic perception of aid to the sick and infirm, some implications of this model will be considered.

---

9. Tendler, Moshe D. (1933). "The Halachik Import of the Psychological State." *Medicine and Jewish Law*, vol. II, ed. Fred Rosner, pp. 67–75. Northvale, N.J.: Jason Aronson.

IMPLICATIONS OF A HEALING MODEL
OF PSYCHOTHERAPY

Maimonides refers to people who stray from the correct path as *cholai nefesh* sick people (*Mishneh Torah, Mada, Hilchot De'ot*, Chapter 2, and, in his introduction to *Pirkai Avot, Sayings of the Fathers*, Chapters 3 and 4). Furthermore, he directs them to wise men whom he calls, "healers of the soul," so that they can be cured. Maimonides' appellation, however, is intended only in a spiritual sense; a sinner is viewed as spiritually ill. This is an important distinction and some writers have not been sufficiently clear on this point, as the following examples will illustrate. Usage of psychological terminology has led a few writers to maintain that Jewish ethicists employed methodology similar to modern psychotherapy to help people achieve emotional stability.[10] This type of reasoning, seizing upon a scriptural or rabbinical word or phrase that seemingly has relevance to psychotherapy and concluding that it alludes to psychotherapy, is misleading. This statement is not to be construed as denying that certain concepts and insights mentioned and discussed in scripture or rabbinical writings are similar to those employed in psychotherapy. The author, in chapters 2 and 3, has analyzed the role of the concept of the unconscious in Judaism and argued that it is a very helpful tool for understanding events recorded in the Bible.[11]

---

10. Applebaum, Seymour W., and Metzger, Alter B. Z. (1977). "Chassidism and Psychotherapy: An Overview." *Intercom*, vol. xvi #20, pp. 15–22. New York: Association of Orthodox Jewish Scientists.

Gottlieb, Mel (1975). "Israel Salanter and Therapeutic Values." *Tradition* 15:1–2:112–129.

Ury, Zalman F. (1970). *The Musar Movement*, ed. Leon D. Stitskin p. 27. New York: Yeshiva University Press.

11. Rabinowitz, Aaron (1979). "Reflections the Concept of the Unconscious in Judaism." *Journal of Psychology and Judaism* 4:1:49–57.

Friedman quotes Hasidic sayings and relates Hasidic tales to show parallels between Hasidism and therapy.[12] Much can be learned from the Hasidic masters. However, treatment of this subject should emphasize that the masters were concerned with moral ethical issues; they did not, on the whole, deal with emotional illness.[13]

There are studies that focus on a perceived similarity based upon shared terminology or preoccupation with subject matter dealing with relations between an influencing agent and an influenced individual. They, therefore, conclude that the subject matter and psychotherapy are governed by the same principles, employ the same or similar methods, or strive toward the same goal. Paley writes about her Talmudic research.[14] The ethical teachings and insights she uncovered are used by her in her therapeutic work. It is gratifying to see the rich repository of wisdom and ethical values in the Talmud rediscovered by a clinician. The use of such insights and teachings is, in itself, accepted procedure. Her examples, however, fail to establish that the Talmudic precepts quoted by her are indeed of psychoanalytic nature. She seems to be unduly influenced by the similarity between Talmudic and psychoanalytic reasoning, leading her to confer psychoanalytic status on Talmudic matter too easily. Her contention that the Talmudic reasoning process parallels the analytic task of seeking contradictions in a patient's reportings is,

———— (1989). "The Unconscious: Its Relation to the Judaism-Psychology Dialogue." *Journal of Psychology and Judaism* 13:3:149–162.

12. Friedman, Maurice S. (1996). "Hassidic Healing and Helping." *Journal of Psychology and Judaism* 20:3:213–232.

13. One finds in the popular literature writers who compare Hasidic teachers to gurus. They view the relations between Hasidic rabbis and disciples as similar to those of the guru and his followers. This is a gross oversimplification and, in some instances, a distortion.

14. Paley, Marlene G. (1993). "Psychoanalytic Teachings of the Talmud." *American Journal of Psychoanalysis* 53:3:247–253.

however, well taken. Others, as well, have pointed to this phenomenon.[15]

Kaplan and Kaplan's papers can serve as a model for research contrasting the Jewish biblical approach and philosophical basis relevant to therapy with other approaches. They postulate that Hebraism is associated with spontaneity and dynamism, as opposed to the Hellenic mode, which is viewed as stable but static. They relate these traits to covenant (Hebraic) in contrast to contract (Hellenic). They proceed to define the parameters of the personality types associated with the above and suggest treatment procedures accordingly.[16] Spero's extensive writings can also serve as a paradigm for research in this area.[17] They are characterized by in-depth analysis of basic issues and are not a simplistic treatment based on perceived similarities between terminology or concepts employed by psychologists and also found in biblical or rabbinic literature.

---

15. Handelman, Susan (1981). "Interpretation as Devotion: Freud's Relation to Rabbinic Hermeneutics." *Psychoanalytic Review* 68:2:201–218.

Jennings, Jerry, and Jennings, Jane P. (1993). "I Knew the Method: The Unseen Midrashic Origins of Freud's Psychoanalyses." *Journal of Psychology and Judaism* 17:1:51–75.

16. Kaplan, Moriah M., and Kaplan, Kalman J. (1979). "The Typology, Diagnosis, Pathologies, and Treatment-Intervention of Hellenic versus Hebraic Personality Styles." *Journal of Psychology and Judaism* 3:3:153–167.

——— (1979). "Covenant versus Contract as Two Modes of Relationship Orientation." *Journal of Psychology and Judaism* 4:2:100–116.

17. See notes 3 and 4 and Moshe H. Spero, *Judaism and Psychology: Halakhic Perspectives* (New York: Ktav Publishing House, Yeshiva University Press, 1980). Dr. Spero has published many other papers which demonstrate his approach.

JEWISH AND CHRISTIAN VARIATIONS
OF THE HEALING MODEL

Knight, a psychiatrist and minister, traces psychotherapy to specifically Christian roots.[18] He writes: "The healing vocation may encompass, but extends far beyond, scientific technology to include a quality of mastery—the gift of healing. This quality is tied to charismatic authority." He quotes Christian scripture (Mark 3:15) as the basis for his statement, "power to heal sickness and to cast out demons." This position is in direct opposition to the Jewish perception of emotional illness and its alleviation. The Torah (Deuteronomy 28:28,34) refers to mental illness as madness; nowhere is it attributed to demons. The sages recognized the emotional basis of mental and indeed even of physical ailments. The Jerusalem Talmud (*Shabbat* Chapter 4, *Halakha* 4) states: "Rabbi Chana, and others say Rabbi Elazar Ben Yaakov, interpret the phrase 'yoke of iron' in the verse (Deuteronomy 28:48):

> and He shall put a yoke of iron upon thy neck, until He has destroyed thee

to mean a morbid preoccupation." The commentary (*Korbon Hoaida*) explains "all sickness stems from unhealthy preoccupation with fears, as for example, fear of the enemy and fear of injuries." This theme is repeated in other sayings in the text.

The model proposed by Knight can lead to a blurring of important distinctions between the functions of religion and psychotherapy. This is detrimental both to therapy and religion. Casting religion in the role of healer, implying that healing is its primary function, is a devaluation

---

18. "The Religio-Psychological Dimension of Wounded Healers." See Chapter 6, Note 1.

of religion. Religion addresses itself to mankind's relation with the Creator and, for a religious person, that is its most significant aspect; saying otherwise is a misrepresentation.

Some theorists, commenting on the relation between Judaism and therapy, have voiced opinions that, in certain aspects, are similar to Knight's position. Much has been written purporting to uncover the Jewish roots of psychotherapy, to cite a few: Bakan,[19] Marthe,[20] Rice,[21] Roith,[22] Yerushalmi.[23] Some see a direct connection, while others dispute this. Such studies add an additional dimension to psychoanalytic concepts and can illuminate rabbinical teachings. Some, however, present positions which, in effect, reduce religion to one aspect—healing. Bakan has this to say: [psychoanalysis] can be understood as a part of, and a contemporary fulfillment of, the style of religiosity that starts with Abraham."[24] This statement, intended to be complimentary to Judaism, actually minimizes it by confining it mainly to its humanistic healing aspects. This trend of thought is similar to that of Fromm who proclaimed that only psychoanalysis is truly religious in the humanistic sense of the word.[25] This the-

---

19. Bakan, David (1958). *Sigmund Freud and the Jewish Mystical Tradition.* Princeton, N.J.: Van Nostrand.

20. Marthe, Robert (1976). *From Oedipus to Moses—Freud's Jewish Identity.* Garden City, N.J.: Doubleday, Anchor Books.

21. Rice, Emanuel (1990). *The Long Journey Home.* New York: State University of New York Press.

22. Roith, E. (1990). *The Riddle of Freud.* London: Tavistock Publications.

23. Yerushalmi, Yosef H. (1991). *Freud's Moses: Judaism Terminable and Interminable.* New Haven: Yale University Press.

24. David Bakan is quoted as saying this in a forum in which he participated (1968). *Psychology and Religion: A Contemporary Dialogue,* ed. J. Havens, p. 96. Princeton, N.J.: Nostrand.

25. Fromm, Erich (1950). *Psychoanalysis and Religion.* New Haven: Yale University Press. See Chapters 3 and 5. See also p. 74 in the Bantam Books edition.

sis has been roundly criticized by Bertocci because it arbitrarily narrows the parameters of religion.[26] Bakan's and Fromm's arguments are anchored in the liberal Protestant tradition which identifies the religious life as the moral life, a position criticized by Kierkegaard, as quoted by Bartley.[27] Their position is not the Jewish perception, which views religion as an all-encompassing way of life.

26. Bertocci, Peter A. (1971). "Psychological Interpretations of Religious Experience." *Research on Religious Development: A Comprehensive Handbook*, ed. M. P. Strommen, pp. 5–41. New York: Hawthorn Books.

27. Bartley III, William W. (1971). *Morality and Religion*, pp. 38–39. London: Macmillan.

SELF-KNOWLEDGE: A CENTRAL COMPONENT
OF THE HEALING MODEL

Treatment of physical ailments is based upon knowledge of anatomy, physiology, etc., plus expertise in the use of remedial techniques. Alleviation of emotional difficulties is dependent upon understanding the intricacies of human nature and the methods employed in making that understanding an integral part of the patient's personality. The role of self-knowledge in therapy corresponds to that of identifying pathology in medicine, and therapeutic techniques correspond to surgery and pharmaceutical applications. Singer writes: "Psychotherapy is dedicated precisely to this aim, to make man comprehensible to himself, to help man fearlessly see himself, and to help him learn that this process of self-recognition, far from producing contempt, implies and brings about the achievement of dignity and self-fulfillment." [28] Self-knowledge means recognizing one's motivations, desires, and goals, and the subterfuges, the self-deceptions one practices to mask the truth from others and more importantly from oneself. Knowing this and taking steps to rectify the lack of self-knowledge is the essence of depth psychotherapy according to Singer. Following the lead of cognitive psychology, academic social psychology has researched the topics of self-understanding, self-awareness, and self-justification very extensively. Their studies have generated many theories; for example, self-evaluation maintenance theory, self-affirmation theory, self-verification theory—all with the intent of explaining the complicated process we use to explain our actions to ourselves and to others. The research has spotlighted the difficulties and pitfalls obstructing true self-perception. Aronson, Wilson, and Akert

---

28. Singer, Erwin (1965). *Key Concepts in Psychotherapy*, p. 65. New York: Random House.

refer to the "illusion of freedom which characterizes so much of our decision-making process."[29] This emphasis on self-knowledge is mirrored in the importance attached to it by Jewish thinkers. This can help explain why some have tended to blur the distinctive nuances that therapists and Judaic scholars each assign to the common terminology used by them.

Bahya Ibn Pakudah cites in his classic "Duties of the Heart" the opinion that philosophy is man's knowledge of himself, and that the understanding of one's physical, emotional, and spiritual self will reveal Divine wisdom (*Shaar Habechina*, Gate 2, Chapter 5). He quotes Job (19:26):

and from my flesh I'll perceive God.

as proof of his thesis.

Rabbi Grodzniski develops the thesis that without an understanding of the inner workings of personality, one cannot comprehend Torah teachings.[30] Two of his examples follow: (a) The Torah prefaces many commandments, *mitzvot*, with the statement that fulfilling them will impress upon the doer the remembrance of epochal historical events, such as the redemption from Egypt and the miracles during the forty years of wandering in the desert—all this so as not to forget Him (for example, Exodus 12:14, 24, 42; 13:9, 10; 14:23, 14; Leviticus 23:43; Deuteronomy 8:2, 11). Notwithstanding the many reminders, we are cautioned not to be haughty (Deuteronomy 8:14) because haughtiness causes forgetfulness. This is so, even for individuals blessed with an excellent memory.

---

29. Aronson, Elliot, Wilson, Timothy D., and Akert, Robin M. (1997). *Social Psychology*, 2nd ed., p. 204. New York: Longman.

30. Rabbi Avrohom Grodzinski (1978). *Torat Avrohom*, pp. 182-214. Bnai Brak: Kollel Torat Avrohom.

It is obvious, reasons Rabbi Grodzinsky, that the issue is not memory per se; rather one must intimately know the workings of the mind to fully appreciate the fact that seemingly extraneous factors can influence memory. (b) How can the contradictions so apparent in man's/woman's behavior be comprehended? How can two starkly opposite traits coexist—the sublime and the earthly? Surely understanding this requires deep understanding of human nature and personality.

The Torah's insistence on complete honesty in examining one's motivation is nowhere better illustrated than in the story of Sarah's laughter. She overheard an angel's prediction that she would give birth, which caused her to laugh in apparent disbelief, for which she was reprimanded. When she denied that she had laughed, the Torah states starkly and simply: "Nay, but thou didst laugh" (Genesis 18:15). The Hasidic master Rabbi L. Eiger explains that she was not aware that she acted disrespectfully.[31] Sarah felt that the angel's prediction could not materialize, due to her unworthiness. It should also be noted that the angel appeared as a human. The Torah, however, emphatically states that she was told that although on a conscious level her modesty dictated her actions, on a deeper level a measure of disbelief had caused her laughter. Self-knowledge and self-awareness are not to be compromised. This train of thought leads us to the issue of the complexity of human behavior.

---

31. Eiger, Leib (1889/1970). *Torat Emet*, vol. 1, p. 11. Bnai Brak: Yahadut.

COMPLEXITY IN JUDAISM AND PSYCHOTHERAPY

A major principle of depth psychology is that human behavior is complex and multilayered. It demands a commitment to delve into motivating factors and personality traits and to follow these insights no matter where they may lead. This, then, is a common factor in psychotherapy and Jewish thought. The Torah's uncompromising demand for honesty in self-understanding and self-knowledge has been noted. Attainment of self-knowledge is difficult because, as stated above, human behavior is multi-layered and complex. Freud compared psychoanalysis to archaeology: a layer is uncovered and a yet deeper level is exposed. The acronym *pardes* (*p'shat, remez, drash,* and *sod*) is a well-known description of the conceptualization of Torah into four methods of interpretation. Torah has also been described as having seventy faces (Eliyuhu, the Gaon of Vilna, in his commentary on Solomon's "Song of Songs"). The need for differing levels of interpretation indicates that human behavior is complex and, therefore, the methodology of interpretation needs to be complex as well.

Rashi's comments based upon the sages' teachings on the word *vayichad* (Exodus 18:9) illustrate the above principle. *Vayichad* conveys Yithro's reaction to his son-in-law's (Moses) description of the punishment meted out to the Egyptians. Moses recounted the details of Israel's redemption from Egypt, including the parting of the Red Sea and the drowning of the pursuing Egyptian army. Rashi presents two meanings for *vayichad*—one (*p'shat*) Yithro rejoiced; the other (*drash*), he was chagrined—literally, his flesh crept with horror. The Torah deliberately chose this word: the usual word for joy is *yismach. Vayichad* was used precisely because of its ambiguity, which is designed to convey Yithro's complex and ambivalent feelings. He was happy for Moses and Israel, but also felt, consciously or unconsciously, sorrow and hurt for the Egyptians, whose advisor he had been for many years. This approach is similar to the reasoning employed by depth psychologists in therapy, for whom the concept of the unconscious is a major determinant of behavior.

Judaic thought is sympathetic to the concept of the unconscious. The confluence of Judaism and depth psychology on this issue, the complexity of human behavior, and the reasoning employed to unravel hidden meanings and nuances of behavior have led some to maintain that psychoanalysis owes a debt to Judaism. Jennings and Jennings feel that the Midrash, the non-halakhic writings of the Talmudic sages, displays the kind of reasoning employed by Freud: "Like psychoanalysis, Midrash is dedicated to explicating and clarifying origins." They call the Midrash the unseen origins of psychoanalysis. This line of argument differs from that of Bakan's central thesis that the content matter of psychoanalysis shows kabalistic mystical roots.[32] Jennings and Jennings are referring to the reasoning process. As noted above, other scholars expressed similar ideas.[33]

Another reason accounts for the complexity of behavior—the phenomenon of inner conflict. Conflict permeates every aspect of human nature. There is no consensus as to the nature of the conflict. Judaism attaches major importance to the tension between the spiritual and the corporeal; psychological theories and systems each have different explanations of the nature of the conflict, but almost all agree that conflict exists and is a constant and inherent part of human nature. This has important con-

---

32. *Sigmund Freud and the Jewish Mystical Tradition* See Chapter 6, Note 18.

33. The ideas and sources in this paragraph are from Chapter 6, notes 11, 14, 15, and 18.

sequences for therapy. It is not sufficient to acquire theoretical knowledge of the complexity and intricacies of the workings of human nature. Emotional well-being calls for knowledge of one's feelings, sensations, and emotions. In modern therapeutic terminology, one must be "in touch with oneself." Our inner conflicts, which dictate self-justification so as to maintain self-esteem, may lead us to engage in suppression of our feelings and emotions. An individual must become adept at recognizing his/her own moods, reactions, and feelings.

Although Judaism's perception of nature of the inner conflict differs from that of various psychological theories, it attaches major significance and assigns far-reaching influence to the role inner conflict plays. The Torah sees people, including those who have attained high spiritual levels, as nevertheless bound to the material self and subject to constant tension between their material and spiritual selves (see, for example, *Duties of the Heart*, The Third Gate, and the Hassidic classic *Tanya*, Chapters 9 and 10). This state of affairs is the reason why persuasive arguments intended to influence an individual to strengthen religious convictions or correct behavior need to be couched in language comprehensible and meaningful to the material self. The Passover seder exemplifies this principle. This most central of all Jewish family rituals is grounded in mitzvot and ceremonies that speak directly to the child and to the more simple facets of human nature. Its important message is not articulated in language addressing the intellect. The symbolism of the matzot and bitter herbs, the four cups of wine, and other distinguishing characteristics is easily comprehended by all and accentuated by the physical acts of eating, drinking, and reciting a straightforward text.[34]

34. Rabbi Yeruchem Levovitz (1966). *Daas Chochma Umussar*, vol. 1., p. 114. New York: Daas Chochma Umussar Publications.

An additional example will further clarify this point:

And He afflicted thee, and suffered thee to hunger, and
fed thee with Manna, which thou knewst not, neither
did thy fathers know; that He might make thee know
that man both not live by bread only, but by everything that proceed out of the mouth of the Lord doth
man live (Deuteronomy 8:3).

Rabbi Kotler singles out the fact that God chose to
bring Israel to a state of hunger first and only then did
He provide manna. Why was this necessary? Would not
the miracle of the daily-provided manna be sufficient to
impress upon Israel the message that He wished to im-
part? Rabbi Kotler deduces that a message is effective only
when the receiver is keenly aware of his/her needs, where-
upon the fulfillment of these needs can and will leave an
indelible impression on the recipient. The mere witness-
ing of a miracle, even one of such magnitude as providing sustenance for a period of forty years for an entire
nation numbering, according to biblical sources, in the
millions, is not capable of branding in consciousness the
effect which God wished to attain. People are a blend of
the spiritual and material; consequently, teaching has to
address both components of the person.[35]

This chapter's intention has been to demonstrate that
some major therapeutic premises are an integral part of
the Judaic perception of behavior. Notwithstanding the
truth of this thesis, the two are not identical. The uniqueness of each and their differences have been described by
May.[36] "It is in this aiding of people to find meaning for
their lives that religion and depth psychology are in part-

---

35. Rabbi Aaron Kotler (1982). *Mishnat Rebbi Aharon*, vol. 1, pp.
8–15. Jerusalem: Mochon Yerushalayim.

36. May, Rollo (1946). *The Springs of Creative Living*, p. 19. New
York: Abingdon-Cokesbury.

nership. The field of meaning in life is essentially the religious area, but the technique of discovering why persons
fail to find meaning—why they suffer hindrances, com-
plexes, irrational fears—is the modern contribution of
depth psychology."

7

Psychology, Education, and Judaism

Professor Safran examines the writings of major Jewish figures with the intent of revealing their relevance and significance for education.[1] Among the issues he focuses on is the relation of the educational principles they espoused to modern psychological theory. This chapter is an attempt to compare and contrast some of the fundamental principles which form the theoretical basis of psychotherapy with those operative in the discipline of education. Specific attention will be directed to the unique aspects of Jewish education.

Education can be characterized as encompassing two main areas of learning: (a) the teaching and learning of factual information (i.e., mathematics, history, etc.), and (b) the teaching and learning of attitudes and values with the goal that they be absorbed and integrated by the individual into his/her frame of thought and hierarchy of values, leading to behavior consonant with those values

---

1. Safran, Joseph (1983). *Studies in Jewish Education.* Jerusalem: Mosad Horav Kook.

and attitudes. This category includes specific political orientations, attitudes toward minority groups, etc., as well as the range of moral–ethical values. Much effort has been expended in researching the psychological processes which account for learning. Many areas of psychology have been tapped to form a coherent, integrated basis for the discipline of educational psychology.

Academic research has primarily been devoted to studying the principles which can account for and explain the kind of teaching and learning described above as belonging to the first category, the acquisition of factual knowledge. At first, research was carried out with animals. Gradually, however, the bulk of research shifted to human subjects. Piaget's studies are a landmark and continue to serve as an inspiration and a model of research and theory. Social psychology has contributed to our understanding of the acquisition of attitudes. Research by Kohlberg, Piaget, and others has enriched our understanding of the stages and laws governing the attainment of moral and ethical values. Their studies have outlined the steps and direction taken by the individual in the development of attitudes and values. Research and knowledge, however, are lacking in regard to how an individual can best be taught so as to imbibe and assimilate the ethical and moral standards deemed as correct and necessary by the community of which he or she is a member. In effect, how does one become an ethical, moral person? Certainly, this is not merely a question of learning of values, but rather of their assimilation and absorption by the individual so that they become part and parcel of his/her personality. Understanding human nature and personality and the stages followed in the acquisition of attitudes and values is invaluable; it does not, however, ensure or constitute by itself a program for best teaching and instilling of said values.

The branch of psychology which seems best suited for

laying the foundations of a program of learning ethical behavior is that which deals with changing an individual's deviant behavior to a mode more acceptable to him/herself and the environment. Psychotherapy is the method used to effect a change in a person's self-perception, a change which necessitates a revision of both the affectual and cognitive components of character in both the conscious and unconscious levels of personality. The way this change comes about and the methods used to attain these goals are a source of disagreement between the various theories of psychotherapy. Each theory is based on its perception of personality and motivation, and the theories differ greatly regarding the proper method of psychotherapy. This discussion is limited to a comparison of the psychotherapeutic methods which emphasize the importance of affect and emotion and in which the concept of the unconscious figures prominently, with educational principles, especially Jewish educational principles. This broad characterization cuts across and includes the methods generally characterized as dynamic, and although Rogerian psychotherapy does not stress unconscious factors, its emphasis on emotion and self-understanding serves to draw it close to dynamic theories for the purpose of this discussion. The chapter does not refer to behavioral psychotherapy or to a pure cognitive psychotherapy.

Adherents of the psychoanalytic method have attempted to apply their theories and methods to educational theory and practice. The history of this endeavor, the problems confronting them, and the areas to which they paid particular attention have been studied and recorded.[2] Rogers has also concerned himself with the in-

---

2. Ekstein, Rudolf and Motto, Rocco L. (1969). *From Learning for Love to Love of Learning: Essays on Psychoanalysis and Education.* New York: Brunner/Mazel.

terface of psychology and education.[3] Others, such as the psychologist Jones and the educator Brown, have also written important books on the topic.[4, 5] These authors, particularly, Rogers, Jones, and Brown attempt to tie in the contemporary emphasis on affect and emotion to education, thereby creating fresh approaches to classroom teaching. They have not, however, addressed themselves specifically to the problem of inculcating morals and values.

Education and psychotherapy are similar in that they view themselves as educational processes. As early as 1916, Oskar Pfister described psychoanalysis as a form of education and suggested that Freud is a great pedagogue.[6] This period marked the struggle that psychoanalysis waged against what it considered suppression by societal mores that favored the natural instincts of mankind. Education was also perceived as oppressive. Ekstein and Motto quote Wittels, a prominent analyst, as follows:

> But the fundamental thought is simple: Leave your children alone. Do not educate them, because you cannot educate them. It might be better if the teachers were to write a thousand times in their copy book 'I should leave the children alone' instead of having the

---

Field, K., Cohler, B. J., and Wool, G. (1989). *Learning and Education: Psychoanalytic Perspectives.* Madison, CT: International Universities Press.

3. Rogers, Carl K. (1969). *Freedom to Learn.* Columbus, OH: Charles E. Merril Publishing Co.

———— (1980). *A Way of Being.* Boston: Houghton Mifflin.

4. Jones, Richard M. (1968). *Fantasy and Feeling in Education.* New York: New York University Press.

5. Brown, G. I. (1971). *Human Teaching For Human Learning.* New York: The Viking Press.

6. Quoted by Ekstein and Motto, *From Learning for Love to Love of Learning: Essays on Psychoanalysis and Education.* Note 2, p. 4. The following quote of Wittels is also from Ekstein and Motto, p. 6.

children write 'During school sessions one is forbidden to speak.'[2]

Further on they quote Pfister, who was concerned with the "faults of parents." They comment that those were the days in which there was a struggle against limits and a constant fear of traumatizing the young, and these concerns were mirrored in psychoanalytic writings on education. Psychoanalytic theory later developed in different directions and, consequently, tended to assert its influence on education in a different fashion. The shift in psychoanalytic thinking on education will be discussed later. It seems almost superfluous to state that the Jewish view of teaching and education is in complete contrast to the psychoanalytic position cited above. Perhaps this incompatibility can account, at least in part, for the antagonistic attitude toward psychoanalysis in traditional Jewish circles. The author, however, does not mean to imply that this is the paramount reason for that antagonism. There are certainly more important and basic reasons which can explain the hostile reception traditionalist Jews give to psychoanalysis. The Jewish position on education, the respect accorded to the teacher, the esteem which is demanded of the student for the teacher—all can be readily ascertained by even a cursory reading of Maimonides (Rambam) and the Code of Jewish Law (Shulchan Aruch). Jewish educational principles are succinctly summarized in Rabbi S. R. Hirsch's writings on the subject. Hirsch writes:[7]

> We are therefore obligated to train the child, at a very early age, in this most important trait. To train him to be able to accept discipline, and to extend his train-

---

7. Hirsch, Samson R. (Nineteenth Century/1958). *Yesodot Hachinuch*, vol. 1, p. 38. Tel Aviv: Netzach Publishing Co.

ing to enable to bend his will to a higher will. Let us not delude ourselves that it's too early to discipline him! If we don't train him to accept discipline, we in effect are training him to be unruly.

Hirsch returns to the subject of discipline in his essay on Mordechai and Esther, "Ma'amar Mordechai." He sees discipline, proper discipline, which is present even when the teacher is absent, and which becomes embedded in the student's personality, as personifying the very essence of Jewish education. Hirsch, however, is not blind to the child's need for autonomy; he does not turn a deaf ear to the child's plea that he/she be granted a measure of independence. He writes:

Educators and teachers who are not sensitive to the child's needs and who violate the child's dignity, teachers who are overly strict disciplinarians—will fail in their educational mission due to the child's sense of independence (p. 66).

In the essay entitled "Education in Infancy" Hirsch again turns his attention to the question of discipline and autonomy.[8] His thesis is that, although factual knowledge is taught and learned in school, moral values are taught, or should be taught, from infancy at home. The school is responsible for the various subjects which comprise the curriculum, but the child's spiritual future is primarily dependent upon the home. He discusses and analyzes the factors which ensure that the home is conducive to fostering the spiritual and moral atmosphere necessary so that the parents will indeed be proper models for their children. Example is the key; education is defined as a process which raises the student's level to that of his parents, his teachers. Parents are exhorted to raise their

---

8. Ibid., vol. 2, p. 43.

moral values and behavior, for only then can the child respond affirmatively to the standards they set. Parents are to discipline their children only when it is in the best interests of the children, not when it merely serves to vent their own exasperation or frustration. Children are to be granted a large measure of independence. On the other hand, education toward self-discipline must begin at birth. These rules are presented to the reader by means of ample illustrations which show a high degree of psychological sophistication by Rabbi Hirsch. His keen eye detects society's propensity to more readily excuse an immoral act than a stupid one. It therefore follows, he reasons, that true morality can be achieved only if the individual can forego, if need be, the approbation of his peers and contemporaries.

As indicated above, psychoanalytic thinking changed, one can say matured, and modified its unbridled critique of education as an oppressor of the child's natural inclinations. Ekstein and Motto describe the change by quoting Anna Freud's views on education in the 1930s:[9]

> She describes the work of Aichorn in his 'Wayward Youth,' and tries to outline an educational task which keeps a balance between the danger of the 'injurious effect of too great repression' and the equal danger of 'the lack of all restraint. . . .' This is a far cry from the previously quoted viewpoint of Wittles in his 'Liberation of the Child,' in which he seems to indicate that the adults, the teachers should abdicate their role. . . . Instead he (the educator) was beginning to stress the creation of an optimum situation in which his orientation was to help the child grow into maturity on a middle road which avoided the pathological traumata of too much strictness as well as unlimited

9. *From Learning to Love to Love of Learning: Essays on Psychoanalysis and Education,* pp. 8–9.

indulgence. . . The first application of psychoanalysis to the field of education, as we note in the new efforts following the First World War, was an expression of protest, a demand for the new. The second step was one in which specific techniques were evaluated through actual application.

Ekstein and Motto then proceed to describe the second phase as one in which the concepts of psychoanalysis were applied in work with individual students as well as in a classroom situation. Stress was laid on the mental health aspects of teaching and learning and on the classroom milieu. During this period, teachers were invited to perceive themselves as educational therapists. Dynamic conceptions of children who were ill were extended to cover the understanding and education of children in general. A third step, which was in the making according to Ekstein and Motto at the time they wrote (1969), differed from the previous phases in that research was directed towards understanding the very process of education itself, in the light of psychoanalytic theory. Field and his colleagues ascribe this development to the new emphases in psychoanalytic theory. They write:[10]

> Freud's initial topographic, economic, and dynamic approaches to the study of learning and development have long provided the basis for study both of learning and emotional factors said to interfere in profiting from instruction. Particularly as derived from Freud's discussion of primary and secondary process, or the means by which ideas become thoughts, much early discussion focused on motives and thoughts, and the extent to which learning was bound in conflict as yet another compromise formation. From this perspective, learning was viewed as problematic: effort expended in

---

10. Ibid., p. 4.

fostering the child's development of reality testing was likely to insure more effective learning in the classroom. . . . With Hartmann's formulation of the adaptational point of view, and White's extension of this perspective in discussion of the development of competence, the relative autonomy of learning was recognized. It became possible to consider learning as a process enjoyable for its own sake, beyond its role as a disguised means for the satisfaction of wishes based on the nuclear neurosis. At the same time, much of the application of psychoanalytic approaches to the study of motivation continued to emphasize problems in learning, rather than intrinsic satisfaction derived from increased mastery.

Ekstein's description of the phases the student passes through as he matures illustrates the stages described in the above quotation. This was not Ekstein's intention. He is referring to developments contingent upon the normal maturing process. Nevertheless, it clearly delineates learning as being, at first, a function of emotional forces in line with classical Freudian instinctual theory which, however, is transformed into an act which is self-rewarding, in tune with Hartmann's and White's ideas. He writes:[11]

At the age of five or six, the child becomes a part of the formal school system. The teachers meet a condition in the child of this age, prepared by his growth process in the family situation. This condition is characterized through his current capacity 'to love and to work,' which is a function of his state of development and maturation. The success of the teacher depends largely on the child's capacity for love and work. As a matter of fact, one must keep in mind that the capacity to teach—as well as the capacity to learn—is a func-

---

11. Ibid., pp. 96–97.

tion of the readiness 'to love and to work.' The teacher-
student relationship establishes the requirements for
a mutually satisfying work experience. The relationship
is based on love in the broadest sense of the word,
which includes natural antagonism and aspects of
anger when the relationship proves unrewarding. The
children quickly realize they must earn the love, the
praise, and the rewards of the teacher. It is because
of this desire of the child to be accepted, to be recognized, to be rewarded, to be marked as a good student
that he is willing to work. For many people, this first
phase of the process never stops. The problem of the
teacher is to develop the process in such a way that
he can reverse the phrase, 'work for love,' and help the
child toward that stage at which he will primarily learn
because of 'love of work.' I suggested earlier that the
first phrase in the process of learning is that in which
one works in order to get love. In this phase, much of
learning might be mastery through repetition. During
this repetition, identification with the teacher slowly
grows. As identification develops, learning based upon
the relationship becomes more and more dominant.
With this identification with the teacher's ways of
working and thinking, with his interests and curiosi-
ties, with his attitudes toward knowledge and skill, the
identificatory processes themselves may lead to the
third phase. Here, the reward and the punishment, the
good and the bad mark, the love or the rejection of a
teacher will not be the dominant feature, or the primary motivation for the child. These factors may give
way to the child's learning to love the work itself, with
its progress, discovery, and mastery of skill and knowledge. Motivation for reward, for love, will be replaced
by inner motivation, and the outer-directed child will
have become an inner-directed one.

The third phase of which Ekstein speaks, the concept
that learning "can be considered as a process enjoyable
for its own sake," is the way Field and his colleagues

phrase it, as quoted above, and is held by Rogers as well.[12] He states unequivocally: "Human beings have a natural potentiality for learning. They are curious about their world." Rogers, however, differs from the psychoanalytic theorists in that he includes both kinds of learning (i.e., factual and values) in his treatment of the educational process. This is so because of the way he perceives therapy and therapeutic change. For him, therapy is based upon and implies a change in the self-concept of the individual. Personality, its development and changes, when they occur, is not a function of the interplay of instinctual elements. Actualization—the inherent tendency of an individual to develop all of his/her capacities—is the key to personality. The same basic principle operates in therapy and in education. Rogers writes:

> Learning which involves a change in self-organization—
> in the perception of oneself—is threatening and tends
> to be resisted (p. 159).

The examples Rogers presents to elucidate this point are those which involve values. It is revealing that Rogers does not even see fit to indicate that. In his essay "Regarding Learning and its Facilitation," from which the above sentence was taken, he discusses both types of learning, factual and values, without commenting on the differences between them. This is so because, for Rogers, there is only one type. All learning is meaningful only when the subject matter is perceived by the student as having relevance for his own purposes, as he explicitly states in that paper. It was noted above that for Rabbi S. R. Hirsch, the two types of learning are not synonymous. One is the province of the school; the other, of the home. A comment on the psychoanalytic approach is necessary

---

12. *Freedom to Learn*, Note 3, p. 157.

at this point. Ekstein, as quoted above, described a phase of the learning process as having its roots in identification—the student identifying with the teacher. The concept of identification in Freudian theory refers to the incorporation of another person's values or characteristics by an individual. It would, therefore, seem fitting that this concept be utilized to account for the learning of values as part of the process of education. However, this does not seem to be the case. Psychoanalytically oriented theorists of education have not attended to this facet in the manner that they have focused on the learning of factual knowledge. An additional comment seems to be called for at this point in order to avoid possible confusion. Rogers also speaks of the importance of the interpersonal relationship in the facilitation of learning, which is the title of an essay in his book, Freedom to Learn. This is not akin to the concept of identification referred to above. Rogers' intention is to single out an empathic interpersonal relationship between teacher and student as crucial for learning by the student. The teacher is not to be perceived as a teacher in the ordinary sense of the word, but rather as a facilitator of learning, one who establishes the proper conditions so that the student can learn. In effect, Rogers is saying that the very same process which causes change in education does so in therapy. The therapist, in Rogers' view, does not directly influence the client; he merely provides the necessary conditions to enable the client to grow, to actualize, to become a more fully functioning person.

Judaism's emphasis on knowledge, learning, and teaching has been well documented: Torah knowledge, its acquisition, is ranked as the most important commandment (*mitzvoh*) in the first Mishnah of the tractate *Peah*. The Talmud is replete with sayings that attest to the high esteem accorded to Torah study and to scholars. Scholars are exempt from paying taxes levied to provide protection, such as hiring watchmen or building a wall around the city. The rationale given is that their Torah knowledge and study is their insurance of safety (Baba Basra 8a). The Jewish personage accorded the highest respect and honor is Moses, who is called "our teacher." Given this basic attitude, it is a foregone conclusion that Jewish educational theory cannot align itself with Rogers' outlook which views the teacher as a mere facilitator. Tradition is the very backbone of Judaism, and the tractate Pirkai Avos ("Sayings of the Fathers") begins by describing how the Torah was handed down through the generations by one illustrious teacher (or teachers) to the other. The Torah explains that the Almighty chose Abraham to be the progenitor of a great nation because he saw fit to instruct his descendants in His ways (Genesis 18:18–19). Rabbi Elazar Ben Shamua stated categorically that the fear of one's teacher (i.e., the respect accorded him) should be as great as one's fear (respect) of the Almighty. He also exhorts the teacher to respect his students' dignity as his own (Pirkai Avos, Chapter 4, Mishna 12): These quotations and many others deliver a clear message affirming the importance of teaching and the position the teacher occupies vis-à-vis the student. The bond forged between teacher and student is that of a father and son (Rambam, *Laws Pertaining to Torah Study,* Chapter 5, Law 12). The Jewish conception of a teacher goes far beyond Rogers' facilitator. This, however, does not imply that the teacher's function is to lecture. The pages of the Talmud testify to the heated discussions between teacher and student, the give and take which exemplifies the nature of Talmudic discussion.

It seems paradoxical that Rogers, who believes that unconditional positive regard of the client by the therapist is the foundation of therapy, does not speak in these terms regarding teaching. This is so, however, on account of his insistence that proper teaching is mere facilitation.

This is not the substance or the proper condition in which love or unconditional acceptance, a concept related to love, can take hold or thrive. Rabbi S. R. Hirsch does speak of the love a teacher should have and feel if he is to influence his student. This love and its expression are not to be compromised, to use Rogers' terms. It must be guided by unconditional positive regard of the child. The teacher must deliberately forget the child's past (in the event that the child was deficient). He, the teacher, must always look to the future.[13] It is both strange and refreshing to meet with Rogers' ideas (i.e., unconditional acceptance, emphasis on the present and future instead of on the past), in Rabbi Hirsch's writings more than a hundred years prior to Rogers. Incidentally, other "modern" concepts are also developed by Hirsch in that same essay, for example, the well-known "Pygmalion Effect," which states that a child will function on that level which he/she perceives as his/her teacher's estimation of his/her abilities and motivation.

It was noted above that the psychoanalytically oriented theorists and Rogers, despite their basic differences, share the opinion that the learner can and should reach a level of learning that is inner-motivated, a stage in which learning is pursued for itself. Rabbi Hayim of Volozhin, in his comments on the fourth Mishnah of the first Chapter of the "Sayings of the Fathers" (Pirkai Avos), writes that Torah knowledge creates a thirst for more knowledge.[14] One's thirst is never assuaged, one drinks of the fountain of Torah and remains thirsty, for this is the very nature of Torah. This phenomenon seems to be unique and confined to Torah study. He does not indicate whether this is so for other branches of knowledge as well; how-

---

13. Ibid. See Note 7, pp. 63–69.
14. Rabbi Hayim of Volozhin (1973). *Ruach Hayim.* Jerusalem.

ever, the evidence, the proofs he cites to bolster his contention, are all within the realm of Torah study.

Psychoanalysis is anchored in the concept of instincts or drives and is, therefore, considered materialistic. Freud's originality and acuteness are demonstrated in his construction of a system explaining man, his achievements, his complexity and diversity as emanating from basic physiological traits. This, of course, is also what many consider Freud's weak point, and he has been roundly criticized by the humanists and others on this issue.[15] Judaism is based on the premise that man is endowed with a spirituality complementing his materialistic, bodily makeup and drives. Altruism, aesthetic values, as well as other values and traits, which are usually perceived as being of a higher nature than base material wants and needs, are regarded as intrinsic to man and, therefore, are not to be explained as a transformation or sublimation of physical drives, as is the case in the Freudian scheme. Nevertheless, one of the outstanding Jewish thinkers of the past generation views some facets of education in ways which at first glance seem similar to the psychoanalytic theorists. Rabbi Yeruchem Levovitz of Mir states that wisdom is not comprehended by the physical person, i.e., man's materialistic nature which lacks the means, the language, to grasp wisdom and to assimilate its teaching.[16] How, then, may man be influenced and guided by wisdom's teachings? The answer to this ques-

---

15. Rabinowitz, Aaron (1989). "The Unconscious: Its Relation to the Judaism Psychology Dialogue." *Journal of Psychology and Judaism* 3:13:149–162.

16. Rabbi Yeruchem Levovitz (1966). *Daat Chochma Umussar*, vol. 1, pp. 212–216. New York: Daat Chochma Umussar Publications. Rabbi Levovitz's and Rabbi Grodzinsky's comments (quoted in the coming paragraphs) were discussed in previous chapters dealing with the unconscious. They are discussed here as well because of their relevance to the subject matter in this chapter.

tion is that learning is to be accomplished through and
by action. Torah's wisdom is transmuted and assumes
concrete forms; these are the mitzvos, the biblical commandments instructing man/woman and guiding their
behavior. Only in this concrete form can wisdom take root
and modify man's nature and behavior. Rabbi Yeruchem
cites the seder night, its laws and customs, as exhibiting
this principle. Contemplation alone cannot ensure that a
Jew will envision himself as if he himself has been redeemed from Egypt. This can come about only by fulfilling the mitzvos of the Passover seder. Even the sage is
enjoined to put aside his learning, his vast pool of knowledge, his erudition, and to participate in the concrete
obligations such as eating the matzot. This is emphasized
by the text of the Haggadah we read at the seder table.
The text is explicit on this point, even the greatest scholars are to leave their study halls, abstain from their deep
theological philosophical debates and discussions, and
read and relate on the seder night the story of the Redemption. This formulation of learning theory frames and
categorizes it as related to and as a function of the materialistic aspects of man's nature. This seems in line with
the psychoanalytical approach. However, viewing it thus
seems superficial. Jewish educational theory views Torah
learning as a spiritual act. It may well be that all intellectual endeavor, being a function of man's higher faculty,
is of a spiritual nature. Man, however, is dualistic; he/
she is materialistic as well as spiritual. Indeed, the yard-
stick of his/her success is whether his/her behavior reflects the spiritual side or, conversely, the materialistic inclinations. This is the raison d'etre of creation. Wisdom
and knowledge are not to be confined solely to higher
faculties, spirituality. They are meant to permeate his/her
other half, to be assimilated by his materialistic nature,
to endow it with spirituality. This can be accomplished,
according to Rabbi Levovitz, only by relating to the body

in its language, i.e., concrete action, concrete mitzvos. The acquisition of knowledge is not rooted in materialism, but its spreading roots, its ability to influence man's behavior is totally dependent upon its settling and becoming part and parcel of his/her materialistic nature. Only then is it considered wisdom. It should be obvious to the reader that Rabbi Levovitz's analysis focuses on "factual knowledge" which will be considered "wisdom" only when it is transformed into behavior congruent with the teachings. This is not easily accomplished. If, however, this does transpire, if man is influenced, then this process constitutes the second area of learning outlined at the beginning of this article.

The practice of psychotherapy assumes many forms. Varying techniques are employed by the adherents of the differing schools, by the disciples of the founders of the branches of this art. These stem from conflicting viewpoints as to the personality and the etiology of psychopathology. There does, however, seem to be a common factor which is paramount in many of the better known dynamic approaches and which is true for Roger's approach as well. Singer writes:[17]

> Psychotherapy is dedicated precisely to this aim: to make man comprehensible to himself, to help man fearlessly see himself, and to help him learn that this process of self-recognition, far from producing contempt, implies and brings about the achievement of dignity and self-fulfillment.

Throughout his book, Singer emphasizes the striving toward self-knowledge advocated and perceived as the goal of therapy. Self-awareness is defined as being in touch with one's feelings, even if this entails a measure of dis-

---

17. Singer, Erwin (1965). *Key Concepts in Psychotherapy*, p. 75. New York: Random House.

comfort, and is regarded as the basis of emotional well-being. This position, its emphasis on self-knowledge and self-awareness means that great stress is put upon the importance of understanding the dynamics of personality motivation. Rabbi Grodzinsky develops the thesis that without an understanding of the inner makeup of personality, one cannot hope to comprehend very many of the Torah's teachings and *mitzvos*.[18] Furthermore, this lack of understanding is an insurmountable obstacle to attaining a high moral and ethical level. In his view, the Mussar movement founded by the saintly Rabbi Israel Salanter, is predicated upon impressing its followers as to the importance of self-knowledge. The changing of one's moral values to conform to the ethical standards of Torah can proceed only if one realizes and is dedicated towards attaining self-knowledge. In effect, the conclusion which seems to emerge from this discussion is that change—the change which takes place in psychotherapy and the change which occurs in the pursuit of ethical ideals—are both based upon self-knowledge and self-awareness.

---

18. Rabbi Avrohom Grodzinsky (1977). *Torat Avrohom*. Bnei Brak: Kollel Torat Avrohom.

8

Ethical and Moral Values

This chapter addresses the interface between psychology and religion as to moral and ethical values. The points where they meet and diverge are many. This discussion is directed toward just a few facets. It would seem that the very nature of religion is such that it includes values and that psychology, the science of behavior, is not concerned and should not be influenced by a value system. It doesn't seem possible to envision a valueless religion. Guttman writes:[1]

> There are religions in which ethics occupies a position of eminence—as for instance in Judaism, where ethics constitutes a determining and decisive principle—while there are religions that lay greater stress on other values. However, there is no religion—or almost no religion—where ethics does not constitute a religious postulate.

---

1. Guttman, Yitzchok I. (1971). *The Philosophy of Religion*, pp. 31–32. Jerusalem: Magnes Press, Hebrew University of Jerusalem.

As to psychology, including both the psychology of personality and clinical psychology, can it justify its claim to objectivity, can it be considered an empirical science if it is connected to a value system?

I will attempt to show that contrary to the above suppositions, it cannot be assumed that values (primarily moral and ethical values) and religion are intrinsically and inextricably linked, or that psychology and values are not. The paths followed by theologians, philosophers, and psychologists relevant to this issue will be traced.

Hick writes:[2]

> It seems to have been mainly in the late nineteenth and early twentieth centuries that scholars discussing religion felt obliged to begin by offering a definition of the word. In 1912, James H. Leuba published a list of forty-eight such definitions, adding two more of his own. More recently, however, there seems to have been a growing—though still by no means unanimous—feeling that the range of religious phenomena is so various and many-sided that no single definition can ever be adequate to it.

Some definitions mention values, others do not. Some call attention to what they term "ultimate concerns" that seem to include values. However, it can be argued that concern with the "ultimate" does not necessarily include ethics and morality. The opposing positions have been documented and analyzed by the philosopher Bartley.[3]

The existentialist psychotherapist Rollo May's description of religion refers to the feeling that life has meaning precisely because it is affirmed through creative living,

2. Hick, John (1989). *An Interpretation of Religion*, p. 16. New Haven and London: Yale University Press.

3. Bartley III, William W. (1971). *Morality and Religion*, pp. 52–56. London: Macmillan.

stressing purpose and values.[4] On the other hand, Whitehead's declaration that religion is "what the individual does with his own solitariness" seems to exclude ethical and moral values.[5]

The American psychoanalyst Mortimer Ostow offers an incisive analysis of the place of morality in the general scheme of religion:[6]

> It is the fact that religion can demand adherence to a code of behavior that makes it possible for religion to recommend and urge morality. Morality is not an intrinsic element of religion (except for the two central prohibitions of incest and murder) but as I mentioned above, was introduced into western religion by means of the spiritual monotheism of Biblical Judaism,. . . In essence, a morally irrelevant act could have as much religious value, that is value in reducing ego pain by seeming to be a transaction with the father God as a moral act. To incorporate moral behavior into religious observance was an act of genius which made religion an institution which not only relieved some of the psychic pain of daily life but also made it a powerful force for social order and cohesiveness.

The above is a clear instance that pristine religion is not to be equated with morality as a given which is almost a priori.[7] Ostow views the confluence, the merger,

---

4. May, Rollo R. (1940). *The Springs of Creative Living: A Study of Human Nature and God.* New York: Abington-Cokesbury.

5. Whitehead, Alfred N. (1926). *Religion in the Making*, p. 58. New York: Macmillan.

6. Ostow, Mortimer (1959). "Religion." *American Handbook of Psychiatry*, vol. II, ed. Silvano Arieti, pp. 1790–1801. New York: Basic Books.

7. An experimental study of this premise was done by Carey Stevens, Arthur M. Blank, and Greg Poushinsky (Spring, 1977). "Religion as a Factor in Morality Research." *Journal of Psychology and Judaism* 1:2:61–80.

between the two as an expression of genius and Judaism's unique contribution to the conceptualization of religion as the theoretical underpinnings of moral behavior. This, according to Ostow, is possible because religion can demand adherence to a code of behavior. It remained for Judaism to link this code of behavior to ethical moral behavior.

OTHER APPROACHES TO THE ISSUE

Ostow's belief that religion is associated with a code of behavior is not universally accepted. Randall is of the opinion that while some religions, Judaism, Islam, as well as the major eastern religions stress behavior or conduct, Christianity in sharp contrast, had come to mean primarily a faith to be believed in, correct orthodox beliefs about God, man, and human destiny.[8] The differing emphases as to the comparative importance of behavior vis-à-vis faith in the structure and composition of religion, illustrate the point that moral behavior, indeed behavior in general, is not essentially an integral part of religion, but is rather an outgrowth of historical developments. It seems appropriate at this point to comment on Randall's conception of Judaism as a law to be followed, rather than a faith to be believed in. It seems more accurate to describe Judaism as an integrated interlocking system of beliefs and conduct. His conception of Judaism lays the groundwork for its being criticized as legalistic, a critique ably repudiated by the American theologian Niebuhr who labels it in the main as nonsense.[9]

The casting together of religion and morality has not encountered universal approbation. Erich Fromm, in his book *Psychoanalysis and Religion*, heatedly criticizes the tendency of both the religious and nonreligious to view religion and morality as indivisible.[10] His critique is based upon his understanding of the difference between ancient Egyptian religion and Greek culture. He believes the former to be a prototype of religion in which the priest is

---

8. Randall, Jr., John H. (1958). *The Role of Knowledge in Western Religion*, p. 15. Boston: Starr King Press.

9. Niebuhr, H. Richard (1963). *The Responsible Self*, pp. 168–169. New York: Harper & Row.

10. Fromm, Erich (1950). *Psychoanalysis and Religion*, pp. 4–9. New Haven, CT: Yale University Press.

the physician of the soul, in contrast to Greece where that function was assumed by the philosopher. He chides the modern world for having abandoned the Greek ideal. He develops the thesis that psychoanalysis can assume the mantle once worn by the Greek philosophers. This, he believes, will benefit mankind by freeing it from the mistaken assumption that living a moral life means living a religious life. He writes:

> I have tried to show in this chapter that the psychoanalytic care of the soul aims at helping the patient to achieve an attitude which can be called religious in the humanistic though not in the authoritarian sense of the word. It seeks to enable him to gain the faculty to see the truth, to love, to become free and responsible, and to be sensitive to the voice of his conscience. But am I not, the reader may ask, describing an attitude which is more rightly called ethical than religious? Am I not leaving out the very element which distinguishes the religious from the ethical realm? I believe that the difference between the religious and the ethical is to a large extent only an epistemological one, although not entirely so (p. 91).

Fromm sees his thesis, expounding a moral code not based in religion, as rooted in and embodying the Greek and Renaissance tradition. He, however, neglects the changes wrought in the conception of religion due to the philosophical questions raised by Hume and addressed by Kant. These questions are related to the problem of the role of knowledge in western religion, which is a major issue in intellectual history. Indeed this is the title of Randall's book, *The Role of Knowledge in Western Religion.* He feels that three main positions have been held in the west as to the place of knowledge and truth in the religious life. He describes the second position thusly:

Secondly, it has been held that Christianity is indeed a revelation of the truth, but this special knowledge is unlike all other knowledge in that it deals with a 'higher realm,' a realm inaccessible to rational inquiry and its methods; or with a quite different aspect of experience from other knowledge . . . Since the time of Kant its proper object has often been held to be the 'realm of values' with which scientific methods cannot deal, as over against the 'realm of fact' which science has appropriate techniques for testing. Since the rise of concern with a 'religious experience' conceived as something quite unique with a distinctive object of its own, 'religious' knowledge has been held 'to be knowledge of the special and peculiar object of this experience— that which the mystic's vision beholds, the 'Holy' or the 'Numinous,' 'Existential Truth' (p. 8).

It is not Randall's intention to maintain that religion's preoccupation with moralilty is a modern phenomenon, but rather that, since Kant, religion in certain circles has been identified solely with morality. This has evolved in order to create an impregnable fortress for religion, safe from scientific onslaught, from the constant change in the understanding of truth. Viewed thusly, Fromm's critique of the state of affairs identifying religion with morality is misguided and inaccurate. He, of course, objects to institutionalized dogmatic religion, but in liberal Protestant circles religion has shed dogma and is identified with morality and ethics. Fromm seems to err on two counts: Firstly, his perception of religion as having always been identified with morality, an identification which he feels hinders progress, is (i.e., the perception) according to both Ostow and Randall, albeit for different reasons, incorrect. Secondly, for many religionists, religion is primarily and almost solely definable as ethical, not dogmatic, a position which is so close to his that one wonders to what he is objecting, and what, therefore, prompts him to cast psychoanalysis as the new religion designated as the guardian of values and the truly ethical life.

Another result of Kant's critiques was the turning, by theologians, to a reliance on "religious experience" as the crux and essence of religion. This was Schliermacher's aim, to free religion from its dependence on metaphysical beliefs. Proudfoot evaluates Schliermacher's contribution as allowing religion to be appreciated as an autonomous moment which is not reducible to science, metaphysics, or morality.[11] In sum, the response to Kant in religious circles was, as Randall noted, to: (1) identify the religious life solely as the moral life, a position, incidentally, severely criticized by Kierkegaard,[12] or (2) free religion from its ties and dependence upon metaphysics and moralilty and root it in human experience. The latter tendency has been channeled into two directions: (a) Schliermacher's and others' insistence on the primacy of affect, on feeling and emotion; and (b) James', and to a greater extent, Otto's approach, emphasizing the cognitive aspects as basic to the religious experience.[13] These have important consequences for understanding the philosophy of religion. The emphasis on subjectivity, the exclusion of the cognitive components by Schliermacher and others, and the concomitant neglect of norms due to the above emphases have been severely criticized.[14] Rabbi Soloveitchik

---

11. Proudfoot, Wayne (1985). *Religious Experience*, p. xiii. Berkeley: University of California Press.

12. *Morality and Religion*, pp. 38–39.

13. Allport, Gordon W. (1950). *The Individual and his Religion*, pp 3–4. New York: Macmillan.

See also: Bertocci, Peter A. (1971). "Psychological Interpretations of Religious Experience." *Research on Religious Development: A Comprehensive Handbook*, ed. M. P. Strommen, pp. 5–41. New York: Hawthorn Books.

14. Soloveitchik, Joseph B. (1983). *Halakhic Man.* Notes to part 1, no. 4. Philadelphia: Jewish Publication Society of America.

———— (1986). *The Halakhic Mind*, pp. 53–55. New York: The Free Press.

views with great apprehension the position which tends 'to deliver philosophical thinking from the yoke of reason' and regards this as one of the causes of the unleashing of the dark forces of this century.[15] He writes:

> When reason surrenders its supremacy to dark, equivocal emotions, no dam is able to stem the rising tide of the affective stream . . . Indeed, it is of greater urgency for religion to cultivate objectivity than perhaps for any other branch of human culture.

Not to do so is to nurture dark passion and animal impulses which can and have caused havoc and devastation. Rabbi Soloveitchik is sympathetic to the concept of the direct religious experience, but anchors it to objectivity and norms—halakha.[16] He elaborates on this theme in relation to prophecy, which he distinguishes from mysticism precisely because it harbors a normative message.[17] To this he adds a most interesting comment: were it not so, he reasons, prophecy would be secretive, egotistical, and therefore, non-democratic. Law, norms, are the factors, the forces that fashion the democratic character of the meeting between God and man. Following this line of thought, it can be argued that the inclusion of ethics and morality in religion is important not only for their intrinsic value, but because they embody normative behavior which is crucial to ensure the democratic nature of religion. No one is above the law and all are equal before the law. This concept, translated and transposed to the theological sphere, certifies the dignity of every man and woman before the Almighty. Tillich is strongly critical of

---

15. Ibid, 1986.

16. ———— (1979). *"Ubikashtem Meshom."* *Ish Halakhah—Golu Venistar*, pp. 128–129. Jerusalem: Histadrut Tziyonit Olamit.

17. ———— (1965). "The Lonely Man of Faith." *Tradition*, Spring 5–67.

the position, exemplified by what he terms the earlier Heidegger, of extreme subjectivity.[18] He also, as we have seen in Soloveitchik's writings, points to the potential for destructiveness inherent in this approach.

18. Tillich, Paul (1952). *The Courage to Be*, pp. 148–149. New Haven and London: Yale University Press.

PSYCHOLOGY: ITS RELATION
TO VALUE SYSTEMS

Modern psychology has also grappled with the problem of the place of values—ethics and morality—in its framework. Psychology, as an empirical science, is a modern phenomenon and, therefore, took pains not to permit values to gain entry into its methodology. This position, it believed, would qualify it to be accepted in the rigorous scientific community. Clinical psychology is an even later development than most other branches of psychology and is rooted in medicine as well as in psychology. As such, it was viewed by its practitioners as governed by the same principle operative in medicine (i.e., that the therapeutic relationship between patient and therapist is not to be influenced by the value systems of either one of them). This dual influence, the empirical legacy of science and the ethical impartiality of medicine, formed the prevailing attitude that moral values were not to be reckoned with in the therapeutic process. Hartmann, one of the major figures in psychoanalysis, writes:[19]

> The only goal of the psychoanalytic method is to undo repressions and all other defenses against seeing unpleasant truth. It has nothing to do with ideologies, indoctrinations, religious dogmas or teaching a way of life or a system of values.

It is, however, questionable whether in reality this goal is achieved or even honored by many analysts. Perhaps this is so because psychoanalytic thinkers did not restrict their theorizing to the etiology of psychopathology. They came to regard their theories as all-inclusive and valid for explaining all of human conduct, normal as well as patho-

---

19. Hartmann, Heinz (1960). *Psychoanalysis and Moral Values.* New York: International Universities Press.

logical, social as well as individual. Definite and specific ideas were held to be the truth concerning human nature; what originated as hypothetical came to be regarded as gospel truth. The usual reservations and healthy questioning which are the hallmark of empirical science were abandoned in a heady rush to embrace psychoanalytic explanations of all facets of culture. Needless to say, these conditions are not conducive to adopting a neutral stance when evaluating or relating to differing modes of behavior, including moral behavior.

Hartmann's position has been criticized on a number of points. Zilboorg writes:[20]

> Psychoanalysis. . . found itself able to go along officially without moral values not because it rejected these values but because it carried them implicitly and inherently as everything human carries them.

He is in effect saying psychoanalysis is a value system. Hartmann would probably maintain that he was not referring to what may be considered universal moral values, but to a specific moral system or systems stemming from a particular culture and unique lifestyle. In whatever fashion this issue may be resolved, it remains a fact that the humanistic school in psychology, the "third force," evolved because of what many considered psychoanalysis' neglect of values. We have seen an example of their thinking in Fromm's proposal to regard psychoanalysis as an exercise in values.

---

20. Cited by John W. Higgins, "Contributions from Related Fields." *American Handbook of Psychiatry*, vol. II, ed. Silvano Arieti pp. 1783–1788. New York: Basic Books.

POINTS OF SIMILARITY

It has been argued that the therapeutic process is based upon the proposition that human dignity is affirmed only if man/woman is allowed and able to freely choose among alternatives. A person who is enmeshed, embroiled, all wound up in his/her emotional entanglements is simply not free. Therapy is to be viewed as bestowing freedom, as releasing the patient from irrational restrictions, restoring him/her to the dignity befitting a human being. Singer asserts that it is essential to the therapeutic process that the therapist believe that he/she, i.e., the therapist, can freely choose, for only then will the therapist be able to help the patient.[21] The patient's potential to achieve freedom is dependent upon the therapist's freedom.

Freedom of choice is also an essential component of the Judaic-Christian heritage. Judaism conceptualizes the meeting of God and man in terms of a covenant which was sealed by ritual entered into freely (Exodus 24:3–9).[22] The concept of free will is the foundation on which the principle of Divine retribution is based. Theologically it is invoked to explain the raison d'etre of creation. Nahmanides, the Ramban, in his commentary (Exodus 13:17), unequivocally states that God created the world solely that mankind can come to realize, affirm, and testify to this. Rabbi M. H. Luzatto, in the second and third chapters of his *Derech Hashem*, elaborates on this theme. God's purpose can be realized only if man, in at least a small measure, can be like Him. This, he explains, means that the spirituality, the goodness that he/she achieves, is to come about as a result of struggle. It is not to be

---

21. Singer, Erwin (1965). *Key Concepts in Psychotherapy.* New York: Random House. This thesis is a recurring theme in his book. See, for example, p. 128.

22. Rabbi Soloveitchik develops this theme in his essay, "The Lonely Man of Faith" (Note 17).

handed on a silver platter. Doing so would demean man/ woman, transforming him/her to a robot-like state.

This analysis defines a common ground on which religion and therapeutic clinical psychology meet. Religion's purpose is to free humanity from being bound and servile to materialism, rendering mankind fit to achieve spirituality. The goal of therapy is directed towards freeing man/woman from pathological defects. Both are concerned with freedom, in itself definable as a value, and furthermore, one that forms the cornerstone of the moral-ethical edifice. This shared area of religion and psychology, both acknowledging and accepting the realm of values, ethics, and morality as relevant and momentous to their fields, is, however, a far cry from Fromm's attempt to view psychoanalytic therapy as a religious process. Others have sought to tie psychoanalysis to religious roots.[23] Bakan has this to say concerning psychoanalysis:[24]

> [It] can be understood as a part of, and a contemporary fulfillment of, the style of religiosity that starts with Abraham.

It has been, I believe, amply demonstrated that although there are similarities and points of convergence between religion and therapy, the above statement and other similar pronouncements are unwarranted and inaccurate. Religion is mankind's attempt to achieve spirituality. Judaism aspires to do this by reaching out towards the Almighty, walking in His ways, and serving Him. Christianity and Islam have accepted this premise, but have

---

23. Robinson, Lilian H. (1986). "Psychoanalysis and Religion." *Psychiatry and Religion: Overlapping Concerns*, ed. Lilian H. Robinson, pp. 1–20. Washington, D. C.: American Psychiatric Press.

24. Cited in *Psychology and Religion: A Contemporary Dialogue*, ed. J. Havens, p. 96. Princeton, N.J.: Van Nostrand.

chosen different methods based upon different beliefs. Although, as pointed out above, the goal of therapy is similar to that of religion, which is to free man/woman, its aim is vastly different. This is mirrored in the therapeutic process. Hankoff writes:[25]

> The psychotherapist tends to define success on the part of the client in worldly terms, with little or no regard for spiritual matters. There is implied in this attitude a tacit rejection of the significance of personal commitment or belief systems. . . . Another pervasive theme in psychotherapy is an emphasis on self-experience and the value of individual expression. . . . Psychotherapy offers as goals such qualities as self-realization and self-actualization.

These therapeutic ideals, as well as others enumerated by Hankoff, emphasize individualism and its satisfactions rather than "a cultural set of values and standards" which is a basic component of a religious system and community.

Another point bears closer scrutiny. If the above arguments are well founded, then to what, exactly, did the humanistic school of psychology object? If indeed dynamic therapy, in contrast to behaviorism, for example, is predicated upon freedom, and its goal is the fostering of a greater measure of choice by the individual, then what fault did they find in psychoanalytic dynamic therapy? It seems that their objection is to Freud's and others' perception of human nature and motivation. Freud's theory is biologically rooted, believing that man's energy and will to act stem from biological needs and drives. To a large extent these theoretical deficiencies were rectified by later

---

25. Hankoff, Leon D. (1979). "Psychotherapy and Values: Issues, Conflicts, and Misconceptions." *Journal of Psychology and Judaism* 4:1, Fall 5–14.

generations of ego and object relations theorists. Nevertheless, distinctly human traits and characteristics such as altruistic, idealistic behavior are accorded secondary attention in their theory of behavior. Esthetics, religion, etc. are considered mere offshoots of sublimatory workings of the dynamic process. To this they object; for them, Freud's conception of human nature is wanting, sterile, and nonsensical.

General academic psychology has also shed its provinciality and deems it legitimate to study phenomena once considered unworthy, or unsuited to scientific study. One of the leading American psychologists expressed this as long ago as 1971. McClelland said:[26]

> I believe that psychology must deal with substantive moral issues, with content. Academic psychology in America has sold out to process—to perceiving, thinking, and adjusting, learning. It is odorless, colorless, and idea-less, concerned only with the how of process, not with what is perceived or learned. . . . Views and values don't get into the research, not openly.
>
> Clinical and humanistic psychologists are in revolt, as I am in revolt, against the lack of substance. Many are the sons of preachers and most of them became violently anti-religious. They formed a new religion out of psychology.

This rather harsh pronouncement graphically illustrates the emotions engendered by the issues raised. It also, however, radiates optimism as to the future of psychological research in religion.

---

26. McClelland, David C. (1971). "To Know Why Men Do What They Do." *Psychology Today* 4:8 January: 35–39;70–75.

9

Religious Experience

THE RELIGIOUS EXPERIENCE: DEFINITION AND ROOTS

The concept of the religious experience and its emergence as a central idea prominent in the religious behavior of people is a late eighteenth century development. It has acquired a respected niche in liberal Protestant theology. Friedrich Schliermacher was the originator of this potent idea which, in the course of time, evolved into many variations.[1] He saw it as a way to protect religion from the critique of Hume, Kant, and other philosophers. The theological basis of religion was predicated on rational proofs from the time of Anselem, Aquinas, and others.[2] These arguments were worn away by new scientific knowledge and philosophical thought. The rapid development of em-

---

1. Schliermacher, Friedrich D. E. (1799/1958). *On Religion: Speeches to its Cultured Despisers*, trans. J. Oman. New York: Harper & Row, 1958.
2. Hick, John (1989). *An Interpretation of Religion*, Chapter 5. New Haven and London: Yale University Press.

pirical science threatened official religion in two ways: (a) it seemed as if scientific findings were in direct opposition to religious tenets; (b) the scientific method, the empirical testing of hypotheses, was viewed as more reliable and closer to truth than relying on scripture or the authority of the church.[3]

The conflict between religion, science, and philosophy, between relying on knowledge gleaned from biblical and church teachings as opposed to knowledge acquired by scientific inquiry, prompted thoughtful people to relate to it. Randall describes at length the challenge posed to the church on many occasions by new scientific findings and philosophical theories.[4] His thesis is that the church dealt with this challenge by reintegrating its teachings with the new scientific knowledge as is evident in Augustine's, Aquinas', and others' writings. Three solutions were advanced, according to Randall, to resolve the particular challenge faced by religion in the eighteenth century. All the solutions were alike in that they called for a reinterpretation of religion. This chapter addresses one of the proposed solutions initiated by Schliermacher and followed by others who adopted his general orientation, but proposed other methods. He viewed religion as representing the emotional aspects of personality, not the cognitive intellectual components. In this framework, theology's task is to provide the symbols to use for expressing the deepest emotions of mankind. The religious experience is the awareness that the individual is intimately linked to the world in the affective realm. This autonomous experience is related to aesthetics, not to dogma, faith, or mo-

---

3. Randall Jr., John H. (1958). *The Role of Knowledge in Western Religion*, Chapter 2. Boston: Starr King Press.

Barbour, Ian (1990). *Religion in an Age of Science*, Chapter 1. San Francisco: Harper & Row.

4. *The Role of Knowledge in Western Religion*, pp. 82–102.

rality. Nature can be characterized and described in scientific empirical terms, but in a symbolic sense it can be understood as the final force, the Creator, etc. The essence of the experience is the feeling of total dependence on this force.

CHANGING CONCEPTS OF RELIGION AS A RESULT OF SCHLIERMACHER

There are two major implications to Schliermacher's thesis. His approach paved the way to consider the study of religion as an autonomous field of study encompassing every mode of religious expression.[5] Scholars studied religion in an attempt to find a common denominator underlying all religions. Although others before his time had pointed out common factors in religions, his thinking created a wholly new discipline, devoting itself to finding the common denominator, the heart of all religions. Schliermacher himself held this opinion. Others followed in his footsteps; the most famous is Rudolf Otto of this, the twentieth century.[6] An offshoot of this trend is the emergence of studies emphasizing the psychological aspects of the religious experience. James' classic is of particular importance and influence.[7] Many others have followed.[8] Other scholars looked to philosophy to explain and interpret the religious experience.[9] The philosophical and psychological studies are similar in that their analysis of the experience is aimed at establishing the validity or nonvalidity of the experience and its implications.

---

5. Proudfoot, Wayne. *Religious Experience*, p. 237. Berkeley: University of California Press.

6. Otto, Rudolf (1950). *The Idea of the Holy*, 2nd ed., trans. J. W. Harvey. London: Oxford University Press.

7. James, William (1958). *The Varieties of Religious Experience*. New York: Mentor, New American Library. It was first published at the beginning of the century.

8. See, for example, *Religious Experience*, Proudfoot, note no. 5, which is a psychological examination of the issue. Note should be made of another study considered a classic:

Allport, Gordon W. (1950). *The Individual and His Religion*. New York: Macmillan.

9. For example: Davis, Caroline F. (1989). *The Evidential Force of Religious Experience*. Oxford: Clarendon Press.

An additional and important outcome of Schlierma-cher's work has been the tendency to increasingly view the religious experience as sui generis. The religious experience is to be understood on its own terms; it is not to be analyzed, or understood on the basis of other disciplines employing their methodology, be it sociological, anthropological, psychological, or any other approach. If, indeed, the religious experience is sui generis, it immunizes religion against attempts to belittle it by pointing out alleged deficiencies arrived at by using the principles and tools of other disciplines. Religion will then find itself strengthened, free from the need to explain itself anew each time it is attacked as a result of new scientific knowledge. The issue whether the religious experience can qualify as sui generis has not been resolved and it does not, at the present moment, seem as if it will be resolved in the near future.[10]

---

10. See Hick, *An Interpretation of Religion*, p. 15. See also: Pals, Daniel L. (1987). "Is Religion a Sui Generis Phenomenon?" *Journal of the American Academy of Religion* LV:259–282.

———— (1986). "Reductionism and Belief: An Appraisal of Recent Attacks on the Doctrine of Irreducible Religion," *Journal of Religion* 66:18–36.

Dawson, Lorne (1989). "Otto and Freud on the Uncanny and Beyond." *Journal of the American Academy of Religion* LVII/2:283–311.

Heschel, Abraham J. (1951). *Man is Not Alone: A Philosophy of Religion*, pp. 221–222. New York: Farrar, Strauss and Giroux, Inc.

THE ISSUE OF A FACULTY
FOR APPREHENDING THE DIVINE

The literature cites four arguments which have been advanced as proof, or at least as establishing a reasonable basis, for assuming that religious phenomena are sui generis: (1) religion is based upon divine revelation; (2) religion is embedded in a unique structure of the human psyche; (3) religion's roots are in the religious experience; (4) viewing religion as sui generis is a heuristic device aiding research into the nature of religion. The second and third arguments have been the most telling and potent in the debate as to whether religion is sui generis.[11] This is so as a result of the tremendous influence Otto's work has had on contemporary theology.

The terms introduced by Otto—*numinous, fascinans, tremendum, mysterium*—are central fixtures of modern religious writing. The sense of the numinous produces in the individual the three feelings of: (a) *fascinans*—being wholly fascinated; (b) *tremendum*—literally overpowered; and (c) *mysterium*—imbued with a sense of mystery. The term *numinous* is meant to convey holiness "minus its moral factor. . . minus its 'rational' aspect."[12] Numinosity is an aspect of the experience or feeling of the transcendent. It also refers to the quality of the presumed reality beyond the experience of the individual. "The overall thrust of Otto's presentation involves not only a state of mind and a realm of value as two distinct realities, but that the first of these is intimately linked to the second and constitutes a form of evidence for it."[13] In Otto's own words "I shall speak, then, of a unique 'numinous' state

---

11. See Dawson note no. 10, Pals (1987) note no. 10.

12. *The Idea of the Holy*, p. 6.

13. Oxtaby, Willard G. (1987). "The Idea of the Holy," *The Encyclopedia of Religion*, ed. M. Eliade, vol. 6, pp. 431–437. New York: Macmillan.

of mind, which is always found wherever the category is applied. This mental state is perfectly sui generis and irreducible to any other; and therefore, like every absolutely primary and elementary datum, while it admits of being discussed, it cannot be strictly defined." [14] He elaborates on the concept of irreducibility, on the experience being, for all its complexity, sui generis and proclaims it is a priori. He believes this is so for both "its rational and non-rational components. . . ."

> The rational ideas of absoluteness, completion, necessity, and substantiality, and no less so those of the good as an objective value, objectively binding and valid, are not to be 'evolved' from any sort of sense perception. . . We are referred away from all sense-experience back to an original and underivable capacity of mind implanted in the 'pure reason' independently of all perception.
>
> But in the case of the non-rational elements of our category of the Holy we are referred back to something still deeper than the 'pure reason,' at least as this is usually understood, namely, to that which mysticism has rightly named the *fundus animae*, the 'bottom' or 'ground of the soul.' . . .
>
> It (the numinous: A.R.) issues from the deepest foundation of cognitive apprehension that the soul possesses, and, though it of course comes into being in and amid the sensory data and empirical material of the natural world and cannot anticipate or dispense with those, yet it does not arise out of them, but only by their means. . . . The proof that in the numinous we have to deal with purely a priori cognitive elements is to be reached by introspection and a critical examination of reason such as Kant instituted.

---

14. *The Idea of the Holy*, pp. 7; 112–113; 114.

Otto clearly states that the experience is qualitatively different from other experiences or feelings and claims it is the basis of religion. This, he posits, is a sui generis phenomenon rooted in a basic a priori faculty of the human psyche. In addition, the knowledge acquired by means of the numinous experience stems from the most fundamental cognitive layers of personality. It is part of the cognitive faculty which, in the Kantian framework, provides the basic cognitive givens, from and within itself.

> The facts of the numinous consciousness point therefore—. . . to a hidden substantive source. . .a 'pure reason' in the profoundest sense, which, because of the 'surpassingness' of its content, must be distinguished from both the pure theoretical and the pure practical reason of Kant, as something yet higher or deeper than they.

THE STATUS OF KNOWLEDGE STEMMING FROM THE RELIGIOUS EXPERIENCE

An additional point needs to be clarified before discussing the religious experience in Judaic thought. Schliermacher viewed the religious experience as rooted in affect, not in cognitive nature. However, others who followed him in the path he opened, perceiving religion as rooted in individual religious experience, increasingly began to look upon the religious experience as possessing cognitive elements, as noted above. They broadened the parameters of the experience to include knowledge of the "object" of the religious experience, that to which the experience relates. They regarded this knowledge as authentic knowledge, no less valid than scientific empirical knowledge. Randall criticizes this position denying this knowledge the legitimacy extended to knowledge acquired or arrived at by scientific methodology.[15] The validity of such knowledge is problematic and the issue has aroused considerable controversy, both sides having detractors and defenders.[16]

To better understand the issues involved, it needs to be emphasized that religious experiences have been, in the main, characterized as mystical. James believes these experiences are personal, not communal and are tied to the person's consciousness when in a mystical state. James then proceeded to describe the experience, delineating four components of the experience, which if

---

15. *The Role of Knowledge in Western Religion*, pp. 94, 108.

16. Hick, John (1988). *Faith and Knowledge*, 2nd ed., p. 210. London: Macmillan.

Swinburne, Richard (1986). "The Evidential Value of Religious Experience." *The Sciences and Theology in the Twentieth Century*, ed. A. R. Peacocke, pp. 182–196. Notre Dame, IN: University of Notre Dame Press.

See also *The Evidential Force of Religious Experience*, pp. 1–10.

present, classify the experience as mystical. Two of these
are essential:

> (a) The handiest of the marks by which I classify a state
> of mind as mystical is negative. The subject of it im-
> mediately says that it defies expression, that no ad-
> equate report of its contents can be given in words. It
> follows from this that its quality must be directly ex-
> perienced: it cannot be imparted or transferred to oth-
> ers. In this peculiarity mystical states are more like
> states of feeling than like states of intellect. . . .
>   (b) Although so similar to states of feeling, mysti-
> cal states seem to those who experience them to be also
> states of knowledge. They are states of insight into
> depths of truth unplumbed by the discursive intellect.[17]

James' position has been critized for being paradoxical. He writes that the experience is so intense that it is
indescribable and yet in his second point, he claims that
the experiences are "states of knowledge." This criticism
has not gone unanswered.[18]

Hick divides the religious experience into three categories:

> By an experience I mean a modification of the content
> of consciousness. . . I now want to suggest a distinc-
> tion between two kinds of such experiences. In the one
> kind the 'information' is mediated through our mate-
> rial environment: things, events and processes in the
> world are experienced as having a religious character
> or meaning in virtue of which they manifest to us the
> presence of the transcendent. For example, a healing

---

17. *The Varieties of Religious Experience*, pp. 292–293. See
Proudfoot's discussion of these points, *Religious Experience*, pp. 119–
154.

18. *The Evidential Force of Religious Experience*, pp. 14–19.

is experienced as a divine miracle. In the other kind, to be discussed in section 5 and often distinguished as mystical, the information is received by a direct influence, analogous to telepathy between two human minds, and then transformed into visual or auditory terms.[19]

In a different chapter (16.5), Hick discusses at length a type of mystical experience which consists of an awareness of union with God, or with the universe, or with the absolute. The second and third types of experiences are considered mystical in contrast to the first type. Hick's categorization provides the framework to distinguish between them on the issue of whether the religious experience is only affective in nature or has cognitive components which provide information or knowledge. The latter two provide information, whereas the first does not, at least in a direct manner. True, the experiencer learns, but knowledge is not transferred from one agent to another which is how he views the second (and third) types.

The contention of some thinkers that the religious experience can and does bear a cognitive message which enlightens the experiencer has to be clarified. What sort of information is imparted? What does the experiencer "know" that he had not known before? James, after he established that the religious experience is varied and widespread, turned to this question:

> We must next pass beyond the point of view of merely subjective utility, and make inquiry into the intellectual content itself. . . but there is a certain uniform deliverance in which religions all appear to meet. It consists of two parts:—
>   1. An uneasiness; and
>   2. Its solution.

19. *An Interpretation of Religion*, pp. 153–154; 165–169; 292–295.

1. The uneasiness, reduced to its simplest terms, is a sense that there is something wrong about us as we naturally stand.
2. The solution is a sense that we are saved from the wrongness by making proper connection with the higher powers. . . . The individual, so far as he suffers from his wrongness and criticizes it, is to that extent consciously beyond it, and in at least possible touch with something higher, if anything higher exists. Along with the wrong part there is thus a better part of him, . . .He becomes conscious that this higher part is conterminous and continuous with more of the same quality, which is operative in the universe outside of him, and which he can keep in working touch with, and in a fashion get on board of and save himself when all his lower being has gone to pieces in the wreck.[20]

Others have proposed and presented other identifying characteristics of the religious experience. The common denominator seems to be an awareness of a relation with a higher being, a greater reality, a presence of the "Real." Neither James nor, for example, Hick, feels that the knowledge gained from the religious experience can be used to "prove" the existence of a higher being. They do, however, maintain that one cannot negate or deny religion's claim to rationality and should respect the claims of those whose religious experience proves for them that there is a God.

---

20. *The Varieties of Religious Experience*, pp. 383–384. See *An Interpretation of Religion*, p. 169. Hick adds other characteristics to those of James.

RELIGIOUS EXPERIENCE: THE JUDAIC VIEW

The basic question is whether the religious experience is as important and influential in Judaic thought as it is in contemporary Christian thought. It seems that although the concept of the religious experience is not foreign to Judaism, it does not occupy the important position it holds in Christian Protestant theology. Traditional Judaism is not based on the religious experience. Halakha, Jewish law, is the paramount feature of Judaism.[21] This precludes viewing the religious experience which is, as we have seen, based on emotion, aesthetics, etc., as being the foundation on which Judaism rests. The primacy of Jewish law is so well established in traditional Judaism that it has led to Judaism being accused of being overly legalistic, a criticism refuted by the eminent Christian theologian Richard Niebuhr.[22]

Another reason why the concept of religious experience doesn't occupy the important niche that it does in Christianity is that the religious experience is personal and subjective, whereas Judaism is communal.[23] Rabbi Mayer Simcha Cohen, in his classic commentary *"Meshech Chochma,"* cites the following verses, and comments:

---

21. Gutman, Yitzchuk J. (1981). *Haphilosophia Shel Hadat*, p. 71. Jerusalem: Magnes Press, Hebrew University.

The Role of Knowledge in Religion, p. 15; Rosenzweig, Franz (1970). *Great 20th Century Jewish Philosophers*, ed. Bernard Martin, p. 130, 143. New York: The Macmillan Co.

Strauss, Leo (1988). *Persecution and the Art of Writing*, p. 19. Chicago: University of Chicago Press.

22. Niebuhr, H. Richard (1963). *The Responsible Self*, pp. 168–170. New York: Harper & Row. This point has been noted in Chapter eight.

23. Buber perceived the Jewish nation as a community which is responsive to the Divine. See Breslauer, S. Daniel (1980). *The Chrysalis of Religion*, pp. 70–72. Nashville: Abington.

Breuer, Isaac (1974). *Concepts of Judaism*, pp. 29–36. Jerusalem: Israel University Press. Also, *An Interpretation of Religion*, pp. 165–166.

Mine ordinances shall ye do, and My statutes shall ye
keep, to walk therein: I am the Lord your God. Ye shall
therefore keep My statutes. . . (Leviticus 18:4,5).

"The verses are in the plural, indicating that the nation, as a nation, is to follow the Torah's ordinances. The
Almighty does not bestow His name on the individual. The
individual is of consequence (in this respect: A.R.) only
when he is part of the community."[24]

The Ramban (Nahmanides), in his Bible commentary,
poses the question. The prelude to the ten commandments
(Decalogue) is in the plural, whereas the language of the
Decalogue is in the singular. He sees this as emphasizing that each person is responsible for him/herself, and
should not be deluded into thinking that punishment will
be meted out only to the community and not to individuals. It is striking to think that an individual might enter-
tain the thought that he/she would not be punished for
an individual transgression. This attests to the importance
of the concept of the community in Judaic thought.

The above seems to lead to the conclusion that the
concept of the religious experience is alien to Judaism.
This, however, is not so. Hick, cited above, defines a religious experience as mystical if information is believed to
have been passed on to the experiencer. Prophecy fulfills
this requirement and accordingly Hick singles out Issiah's
prophecy as a mystical religious experience.[25] This seems

---

24. Commenting on Leviticus 23:21, he stresses that part of the
six hundred and thirteen commandments of the Torah are indicative
of God's intent to mould and unify the Jewish nation because He
bestows His name on the nation. Their function is to unify them under one banner, that of serving God as a nation. Other mitzvot (commandments) bind each individual to Him directly. For example, the
Sabbath binds each individual directly to God, the Holidays bind the
individuals to one another forming a community to serve Him.

25. *An Interpretation of Religion,* pp. 165–166.

to contradict what has been shown, that Judaism is a communal experience, whereas prophecy is perceived an individualistic experience. Rabbi Soloveitchik, however, in his essay "Lonely Man of Faith," develops the theme that prophecy is a communal phenomenon.[26] The prophet must bear in mind that he/she is only a messenger. Moreover, every relationship with God, if it is to be redeeming, must contain a normative ethical message. If this is not so, even prophecy, in spite of its sublimity, cannot be considered a manifestation of the covenant between God and His people. Covenant implies a free acceptance of responsibilities, and this is what distinguishes it from an intuitive mystical experience. He sees prophecy as bound to its normative message and, therefore, not in essence a classical mystical experience. Prophecy according to him is: (1) a bearer of a normative message; (2) a communal phenomenon. The idea that prophecy, in the main, is directed to the community and that the prophet is the lesser figure is supported by the sages' comment. When Israel sinned by adoring the golden calf, Moses, who was in the process of receiving the tablets of the law from God, was told to descend Mount Sinai (Exodus 32:7). Rashi quotes the sages who interpreted the command to Moses to descend as also indicating that he would lose his special status: "I bestowed greatness upon you only for Israel's sake." Israel's sinning caused Moses to forfeit (for that period) his unique position. Bestowing upon Moses the gift of prophecy was not for his personal enrichment, but to bring God's message, the Torah, to Israel. This analysis of prophecy excludes viewing it as a mystical religious experience and with it the idea that the concept of the religious experience has a respected place in Jewish thought.

---

26. Soloveitchik, Rabbi Joseph B. (1965). "The Lonely Man of Faith," *Tradition*, Spring, pp. 5–67.

Although the arguments presented above seem well founded, nevertheless one cannot conclude that the concept has no place in Judaism. True, Judaism is not to be based upon this concept, but the religious experience can function as a source of spiritual enrichment for individuals. Prophecy, although primarily a communal experience, can also be an individual personal phenomenon, as Rabbi Soloveitchik notes in his essay.[27] He directs our attention to Maimonides' Code of Law (*Hilchot Yesodai Hatorah* 7:7) and to *A Guide to the Perplexed* (2:37) which state that prophecy to an individual, not containing a normative message to the community, is possible. This bears explaining. The sages (Talmud, Megillah 14A) inform us that during the course of the centuries, there were over 1,200,000 prophets, twice the amount of Israelites who were redeemed from Egypt. However, only those whose prophecies were relevant to coming generations, as well as to the immediate generation, were recorded. To summarize, the Talmud teaches and this is so noted in the Maimonidean code, that: (a) there were communal prophecies, i.e., directed to the community, which were not recorded because they lacked relevance for succeeding generations; (b) there were individuals who were blessed with the gift of prophecy to enhance and further their spiritual intellectual enrichment. The Rambam specifically states that this type of prophecy broadened and deepened the prophets' wisdom and knowledge. The kabbalist Rabbi

---

27. Mention should be made of a phenomenon which is unique to Judaism: a national or nationwide religious experience. All the Israelites were present at Mt. Sinai. God spoke to all of them. All attained prophecy for that sequence in time, for that event. This idea can be elaborated and note be made of the fact that the redemption from Egypt, the miracles in the desert were all national experiences. Indeed this theme, stressed by Rabbi Yehuda Halevi, the most famous Jewish poet of the Middle Ages and one of its most eminent philosophers, is one of the theoretical pillars of his classic work, the *Kuzari*.

Moshe C. Luzzatto, "Ramchal," agrees with the Rambam in that he also believes that the prophet and the person who attains "Ruach Hakodesh" (a gift lesser than that of prophecy attainable even in this age, i.e., after prophecy was terminated, which according to Jewish tradition occurred at about the time of the destruction of the first, Solomon's, temple) becomes privy to hidden knowledge. Prophecy is described as "devaikut," literally cleaving unto God. Devaikut is the ultimate in spirituality attainable in this world. Knowledge of the divine is intertwined with the state of devaikut.[28]

28. Luzzatto, Moshe C. (1981). *Derech Hashem*, pp. 103–105. Jerusalem: Feldheim. Popularly known as the "Ramchal," he lived and wrote at the beginning of the eighteenth century. His ethical work, *Mesillat Yeshorum*, is a classic and one of the most studied ethical treatises. He is also considered by many as one of the fathers of modern Hebrew literature.

DEVAIKUT, CLEAVING, AND ITS RELATION TO THE RELIGIOUS EXPERIENCE

Rabbi Luzzatto, the "Ramchal," ties cognitive knowledge to devaikut. An explanation of devaikut is called for. The Torah mentions devaikut a number of times. For example: Deuteronomy 4:4; 11:22; 13:5. Rashi notes the sages' interpretation of the concept in two places. In his commentary to Deuteronomy 13:5, he writes: "Cleave unto His ways, do acts of lovingkindness, bury the dead, visit the sick as did the Holy One." In Deuteronomy 11:22, he writes: "Is it possible to cleave unto Him? He is a consuming fire! What is meant is to cleave unto the wise pious scholars and their students." A third interpretation is found in the Sifri (a compilation of the sages' comments on Deuteronomy 13:5, paragraph 60). "Separate yourselves from idolatry and cleave unto Him." The common denominator of the three interpretations is that they are not mystically oriented; they do not imply a direct relationship with Him, but a closeness achieved by various methods. There are other interpretations which present the concept of devaikut differently. The Ramban (Nahmanides) in his commentary (Deuteronomy 6:13) writes:

> It is possible that what is meant is that you should constantly remember Him and His love, your thoughts should not leave or digress from Him even when you travel, retire at night and arise in the morning. So much so that even when you converse with others you do so overtly with your lips and tongue, but your heart is not with the other but with God. These individuals can be viewed as even in their lifetime ensconced in the wreath of life, and in them rests the Shechina (Holy Spirit) as was hinted at in the Kuzari, and was already noted by me in my commentary on the laws pertaining to incest.

The Ramban is referring to his comments on Leviticus 18:4. In those comments the Ramban rates, on a sliding scale, the rewards of the just. On the first rung of the ladder are those individuals who obey the commandments, the *mitzvot*, for ulterior reasons—to obtain the reward. They will be rewarded with the benefits of life, wealth, and be respected in this world. Above them are those who heed God's commandments because they aspire to eternal life. They serve God out of fear; they will be rewarded as they wish with eternal life. On the third rung of the ladder are those who serve God lovingly, while at the same time living a normal daily routine life. The highest ratings are held by those who "forego all contact with this world, don't attend to worldly material desires as if they themselves are not corporeal. All their thoughts and desires are channeled towards spirituality as was the case with Eliyuhu (Elijah). Their spirit is in a sense bound to Him. They will live forever as related by scripture and known through tradition. This also was the case with Chanoch (Genesis 5:24)."

The Ramban's interpretation of devaikut is, if course, different from the previously mentioned interpretations. His comments touch on the mystical elements of the concept. The body will not experience death; the level of spirituality is such that even material substances will acquire spiritual characteristics, resulting in everlasting life. The Ramchal expresses a similar idea in his *Path of the Just* (*Mesillat Yeshorim*), chapter 26. He lists, in detail, all the traits required to achieve maximum holiness and then describes the person who has managed to reach this height:

> And then he will be like an angel. All his actions and behaviors, even common ordinary acts, will be considered as sacrifices on the altar.

The founder of *Chabad Chasidus* (*Hasidut Lubavitch*) in *Tanya* (Chapter 46) differentiates between two types of devaikut. One is described metaphorically as a kiss, the other a hug. The first higher level is attained by studying Torah, the second by fulfilling the Torah's mitzvot. His description of the spiritual bonds formed by studying and performing mitzvot are couched in language similar to that of the Ramban and Ramchal. His division of the concept of devaikut into two aspects allows a theoretical framework by which to identify or characterize different interpretations of devaikut. It teaches that the concept has many facets and a pluralistic model is an accurate description of the concept. This is not surprising. Simon the Just taught (*Sayings of the Fathers, Pirkai Avot* 1:2) that the world rests on three pillars. The study of Torah, worship in the temple (and after its destruction, prayer), and acts of loving-kindness. In similar fashion the concept of devaikut can and does contain different aspects.

THE RELATION BETWEEN THE STUDY OF TORAH, PRAYER, AND DEVAIKUT

Prayer is described by the sages as serving God with the heart (Talmud, Taanit 2A). Rabbi Hayim of Volozhin (*Nefesh Hachayim*, Gate 2, Chapter 11) writes that the essence of prayer is the wish to grant or confer greater power to holiness. The world is both pure and impure, prayer strengthens holiness. One's sole guide in praying is to achieve this end, to eradicate defilement and impurity and thereby hasten God's kingdom in this world. Prayer has the ability to somehow connect with higher levels of holiness and have them reach out and purify our world. One should not think in terms of personal needs when praying. He asserts that the perception of prayer as devaikut is more than a mere metaphorical appellation. One prays with the *nefesh* (soul); therefore, when praying one should separate the physical, the body, from the soul to such an extent that the person will wish that the nefesh leave the body and ascend with the prayer. Furthermore, the level of spirituality to be aspired to in prayer is such that the person should turn into a vessel to be activated by God. He teaches that the opening sentence to the main prayer, *tefilat amidah*—the eighteen benedictions, in which the individual asks God to "open" his lips—is not meant to be a metaphor. One can actually reach a level of holiness of such intensity that the prayers will flow from one's lips (Gate 2, Chapters 14, 18).

At this point, a comparison can be made between the Jewish perception of prayer and that of James. James writes:

> That prayer or inner communion with the spirit thereof—be that spirit 'God' or 'law'—is a process wherein work is really done, and spiritual energy flows

in and produces effects, psychological or material,
within the phenomenal world.[29]

The sages and Jewish thinkers quoted above stress
points not attended to by James. Although he is willing
to grant the possibility that prayer has actual effects, he
is prudent and qualifies his statement by adding that the
effects may take place only in the psychological realm.
Nevertheless, there is a similarity between the two approaches in that James, as in the Jewish view, sees prayer
as linking humanity to the unknown, unseen spiritual
world.

The relation between the study of Torah and devaikut
remains to be explained. The spirituality of prayer which
is man's/woman's reaching out to God, supplicating and
beseeching Him, is self-evident. Although one can understand the reasons for the supreme importance that learning Torah occupies in Judaism, it is not clear how this
cognitive act can be considered the epitome of devaikut.
Rabbi Hayim of Volozhin writes that when studying Torah, there is no need to consciously seek God's closeness
or attachment—learning Torah is itself devaikut. The wish
to understand Torah, wanting to be familiar with it and
desiring to be knowledgeable in Torah studies, is considered leshma (i.e., for the glorification of His name). This
is so because He and His will are one and inseparable.
Every dictate (mitzvah) is a manifestation of His will. Every word of Torah uttered by the learner is at that moment uttered by the Almighty as well (Gate 4, Chapter 6).
In Chapter 20, he extols the virtues of the learner, of the
scholar, quoting the sages that the wise man, the scholar,
is on a higher level than that of the prophet. The Tanya
(Chapter 26) also writes in the same vein, stressing the
same point that the Law, halakha, is the expression of

---

29. The Varieties of Religious Experience, p. 367.

God's will. The intellectual act of learning is considered devaikut. This singular Jewish emphasis is a novel interpretation of being close to God and a unique perception of the religious experience.

An additional illustration will serve to further clarify this point. An individual who constantly learns to the extent that he is in the category of *Torato Umanuto* (a category not operative in our age as regards the application of the law here discussed), is exempt from fulfilling the mitzvot including prayer. Rabbi Kook explains that the spirituality attained by the constant learning is so intense and deeply ingrained that there is no need to elevate the emotions through the medium of prayer. The pinnacle has already been reached.[30] This is a clear exposition of the principle that, in Judaism, the cognitive act of Torah study influences and purifies the emotional side of man.

---

30. Kook, Rabbi Avrohom Y. (1962). *Seder Tefillah Im Olat Reiyah,* p. 22. Jerusalem: Mosad Horav Kook.

FURTHER EXPLORATION OF THE JEWISH PERCEPTION OF THE RELIGIOUS EXPERIENCE

Rabbi Soloveitchik addresses the issue of the religious experience in a number of his publications. He analyzes the different philosophical systems and their attempt to understand man's relation to and understanding of the divine. The classical method is to try and show, by logical proofs, the existence of God and other theological principles. Modern philosophical thinking negates this approach. Rabbi Soloveitchik comments that this development, which ostensibly set out to refute the validity of logical proofs of theological principles, ended by strengthening belief. Although logical proofs are not possible according to this approach, it claims that they are not needed. It proclaims that proof is based upon direct experience:

> Just as when seeing a tree we conclude that it has roots underneath in the earth, perception of the trunk is also perception of existing roots, in like fashion man is not in need of logical propositions in relation to God.

He quotes the famous midrash (Aggadic saying) in which Abraham reasoned that it is not possible that a mansion all lit up is not someone's property and has not been constructed by a person, similarly it's not possible that the world evolved by itself without a creator. He goes on to say:

> ... this is not meant to be a logical proof, but rather a proclamation that man sees the divine in every aspect of creation.[31]

---

31. Soloveitchik, Joseph B. (1979). "*Ubikashtem Mishom*" *Ish Halocho Golu Venistar*, ed. S. Schmidt, p. 127. Jerusalem: Histadrut Ziyonit Haolomit.

Rabbi Soloveitchik seems to be referring to those thinkers who developed the concept of the religious experience to buttress religion. He, however, distinguishes between Schliermacher whose subjective approach he sees related to Kierkegaard, Sabatier, and Hermann who are characterized as adherents of the subjective school. The approach he discusses and prefers seems that initiated by Otto. He argues that Maimonides (Hilchot Yesodai Hatorah, chapter 1) accepted this approach. Maimonides writes that "the basis of all and the pillar of wisdom is to know that there is a first cause (the Creator: A.R.) and that everything in the universe emanates from the truth of His being." Maimonides, argues Rabbi Soloveitchik, does not present logical proofs for this statement although he was not averse to doing so, to present proofs based on logic in the classical manner. Here the Rambam asserts that this knowledge, i.e., that there is a first cause is based upon ontological direct recognition that nothing exists without God. Rabbi Soloveitchik's position is explicit; the religious experience provides knowledge. In another of his writings, he takes Otto to task for not being sufficiently aware and attuned to the cognitive significance of the religious experience. Otto did not note the overriding desire humans have to know, to understand, to fathom the unfathomable.

> Moses sees the burning bush. On the one hand, confronted by the mysterium tremendum, he hides his face in fear of looking upon God; but, on the other hand, he says, 'I will turn aside now and I will see this great sight as to why the bush is not consumed.' The homo religiosus senses the insolubility of the mystery, but nonetheless yields to an irresistible temptation to solve it.[32]

---

32. ——— (1986). *The Halakhic Mind,* pp. 119–120. New York: Seth Press.

Another facet of the religious experience is analyzed by Rabbi Soloveitchik. He quotes the kabbalists, who taught that the cosmos is an offshoot of the divine. An autonomous creation is an impossibility; there is no entity but God. Although what we see seem to be independent, autonomous entities, in reality they are but a function of what they, the kabbalists, term *tzimzum*—a mysterious process in which it seems to the viewer as if the Creator distances Himself from His creation. In His presence, nothing can exist; everything is absorbed by Him. In reality, however, there is nothing but the Almighty. It follows that drawing closer to Him, cleaving unto Him, is, in a sense, self-destruction.[33]

This analysis elucidates why the sages chose to emphasize those aspects of devaikut which do not contain mystical elements. The mystical, the esoteric, is not usually spoken of by the sages in open fashion. They prefer, in their interpretations, to speak openly about the rational, the easily understood. Although there is no question but that devaikut also means those aspects which the Ramban and others discuss, they preferred not to stress and openly emphasize those interpretations. They chose, therefore, to explain devaikut as, for example, walking in His ways. We, however, are bound to explain the Ramban's and others' interpretations which do stress the mystical. This issue can be resolved by invoking another principle discussed by Rabbi Soloveitchik, a principle noted by others as well, which he saw fit to dwell upon at length. He notes that the Greek Plotonius and his followers wished to immerse themselves completely in the Divinity and become one with it. They chose to follow the path of *via purgativa* which leads to *Unio Mystica*. This path enables the individual to lose his/her uniqueness, his/her identity to experience total union with God. This, says Rabbi

---

33. "Ubikashtem Mishom," pp. 167–190.

Soloveitchik, is not the Jewish approach. It does not view with favor unity in which the individual, in effect, ceases to be. Judaism does not speak of union, but of cleavage, devaikut. The individual is not absorbed, only bound. The Ramban and Ramchal understood devaikut to mean, in addition to the interpretations given by the sages, the experience of becoming closer and cleaving unto Him, but not necessarily becoming totally absorbed by the Divinity.[34] This is to be understood as referring to the individual's perception of what constitutes closeness, not the actual state of events. In reality, there is nothing but Divinity. All that exists has come about through a process, as noted above, called *tzimzum*. This allows us to perceive nature, people, ourselves as autonomous entities, a perception valid for the state of devaikut as well.[35]

---

34. Ibid, pp. 189–190. Barbour, *Religion in an Age of Science*, pp. 47–49, quotes Ninian Smart who distinguishes between numinous encounter and mystical union. In mystical union the distinction between subject and object is overcome in an all-embracing unity beyond all personal forms. To this Rabbi Soloveitchik would object. See Hick, *An Interpretation of Religion*, pp. 292–295. See also Proudfoot, *Religious Experience*, p. 122.

35. Rabbi Mayer S. Cohen (*Meshech Hachochma* Genesis 12:7) expounds a principle far reaching in its theoretical consequences. It is axiomatic that the material hinders the spiritual. An individual must overcome and, if possible, purify bodily wants and drives. Spirituality is measured by the individual's success in that task. Rabbi Mayer Simcha writes that not only can the deleterious influence of the material be eliminated but the body, if properly purified, can become an instrument to enlarge the spiritual realm. He likens the body to a microscope, serving to enlarge and enhance spirituality and holiness to a degree which would not be possible without it. He interprets the verse (Job 19:26) "from my body I will view God" in this fashion.

IS THERE IS A FACULTY
FOR APPREHENDING THE DIVINE?

Rabbi Mayer Simcha, in at least two comments, states that the human soul possesses a faculty for perceiving the Divine. This is embedded in the human mind as is other a priori knowledge, for example, that the whole is greater than any of its parts.[36] It will be shown that Judaism regards the soul as a spiritual segment of the Divine. Accepting this must invariably lead to the position that it, the divine soul, can apprehend Divinity.

The Ramban, in his commentary on the Bible (Leviticus 18:29), states that the soul is eternal. This, he says, explains why the Torah does not specifically mention that the reward for obeying God is eternal life. The Ramban says that this is the normal state of affairs. The Creator "breathed into his nostrils the breath of life" (Genesis 2:7). The Torah does, however, have to inform us that if man sins, God will alter the normal state and cut off the soul from its source.[37]

The concept that the soul is a spiritual segment of the Almighty is articulated by a number of thinkers. Rabbi Hayim of Volozhin discusses this in "Nefesh Hachayim" (Gate 1, chapters 4-7 and chapter 15; Gate 2, chapter 14).

---

36. *Meshech Hachochma*, Genesis 12:7;Deuteronomy 11:14.

37. An interesting application of the concept that the soul is divine and eternal is made by the *"Arugat Habosem"* (quoted in *Techailat Mordechai* Leviticus 26:11, published in Jerusalem by Levin Epstein Publishing House) to the verse "And I will set my tabernacle among you, and my soul shall not abhor you." This verse is perplexing, its difficulty noted by the Ramban. Can God's reward for obeying Him be that He will not abhor Israel? The *"Arugat Habosem"* explains it thusly: God's placing His tabernacle signifies that Israel is following in His ways. In that situation, purity and holiness are such that it may come to pass that the souls of the righteous will naturally gravitate towards their source—to God—and will leave their earthly bodies. The Torah assures us that this will not be.

Rabbi Shneur Zalman, in his Tanya chapters 2, 35, and 46, discusses this at length.[38] These and other authors develop the theme that the divine soul is capable of apprehending Divinity as a function of its very nature.[39] This also deepens our understanding of the sages' teaching that the embryo is taught Torah. This is explained by Rabbi Avrohom who quotes his brother, the Gaon of Vilna and the "Alshich" that every person has a share of Torah which is specific to his soul. This is the share taught in the embryonic state and is the foundation for the belief that if the person studies properly, he is assured that knowledge will not elude him. This is so because he is retrieving that which he had already had and is why the sages say "if you worked hard, you will find." The term "find" is used because the Torah was lost at birth, but it can be "found" again by studying diligently. We are taught an important principle. The soul can apprehend divinity and it has imprinted on it cognitive knowledge—Torah.[40]

There is an additional aspect to the Jewish perception of the religious experience which seems unique to Judaism. The overwhelming experience described by Otto is based upon the affective components of the soul and the cognitive traits of the mind when confronted with the Divine. The experience so eloquently described by Otto is basically a feeling of nothingness when the person finds

---

38. Rabbi Hayim Vital, the foremost disciple of the "Ari" and the disseminator of his Kabbalah doctrine, utilizes the ideas that the soul is divine to explain prophecy (*Shaarai Kedusha*, Part 3, Gates 3–8).

39. Karelitz, Rabbi Avrohom Yeshaya (1974). *Chazon Ish Taharot, Emunah Ubitochon*, Chapter 1:9. Bnai Brak: A. Karelitz.

See also:

Kook, Rabbi Avrohom Y. (1967). *Adar Hayokor*, p. 30. Jerusalem: Mosad Horav Kook.

—— (1971). *Musar Ovicha*, p. 98. Jerusalem: Mosad Horav Kook.

40. Hagra, Rabbi Avrohom Achi (1971). *Maalot Hatorah Amudai Hatorah*, pp. 221–222. Jerusalem: Keter Torah.

himself/herself facing the majesty of God. Jewish tradition teaches that in addition to the above, humans were designated by the Almighty to be His partners. People were entrusted with the sacred mission of being the driving force of the universe. A person's behavior determines the nature of the universe.[41] The person has within him/her the power to build or destroy. This, of course, is not apparent to the human eye. This awesome responsibility given to mankind impresses upon the individual the trust and love extended to the human race by the Creator. In spite of man's frailty, he/she becomes a partner, the soul—a segment of the Creator—and his/her actions influence and determine universal destiny. This extends the parameters of the religious experience in a direction not mentioned by others and can be perceived as the unique Jewish stamp upon the concept of the religious experience.[42]

---

41. Rabbi Hayim of Volozhin, in his classic *Nefesh Hachayim*. This is the dominant theme in his work. See, for example: Gate 1, Chapters 4–7, and Gate 2, Chapter 14.

42. See also:

Safran, Bezalel (1988). "Maharal and Early Hasidism." *Hasidism: Continuity or Innovation*, ed. Bezalel Safran, pp. 47–144. Cambridge, MA: Harvard University Press.

Index

About the Author

Aaron Rabinowitz was born in New York City. He attended City College of New York, where he received an M.A. in clinical school psychology. His extensive Jewish education includes advanced talmudic studies at the yeshiva in Lakewood, NJ. Dr. Rabinowitz currently serves as a member of the psychology faculty at Bar-Ilan University in Israel, where he teaches courses on therapy and diagnostics, as well as giving seminars on personality. Dr. Rabinowitz's research interests and publications are in the fields of aggression, imagination, and social schemata. Dr. Rabinowitz also maintains a small private practice as a clinical psychologist. He and his wife, Shoshana, have four married children and reside in Israel.